Migrating ASP.NET Microservices to ASP.NET Core

By Example

Iris Classon

Apress®

Migrating ASP.NET Microservices to ASP.NET Core: By Example

Iris Classon
29 Gothenburg, Sweden

ISBN-13 (pbk): 978-1-4842-4326-8   ISBN-13 (electronic): 978-1-4842-4327-5
https://doi.org/10.1007/978-1-4842-4327-5

Copyright © 2019 by Iris Classon

Managing Director, Apress Media LLC: Welmoed Spahr
Acquisitions Editor: Joan Murray
Development Editor: Laura Berendson
Coordinating Editor: Jill Balzano

Cover image designed by Freepik (www.freepik.com)

Distributed to the book trade worldwide by Springer Science+Business Media New York, 233 Spring Street, 6th Floor, New York, NY 10013. Phone 1-800-SPRINGER, fax (201) 348-4505, e-mail orders-ny@springer-sbm.com, or visit www.springeronline.com. Apress Media, LLC is a California LLC and the sole member (owner) is Springer Science + Business Media Finance Inc (SSBM Finance Inc). SSBM Finance Inc is a **Delaware** corporation.

For information on translations, please e-mail rights@apress.com, or visit http://www.apress.com/rights-permissions.

Apress titles may be purchased in bulk for academic, corporate, or promotional use. eBook versions and licenses are also available for most titles. For more information, reference our Print and eBook Bulk Sales web page at http://www.apress.com/bulk-sales.

Any source code or other supplementary material referenced by the author in this book is available to readers on GitHub via the book's product page, located at www.apress.com/9781484243268. For more detailed information, please visit http://www.apress.com/source-code.

Printed on acid-free paper

*To the .NET community, my second home
and whose never-failing encouragement helped
keep my fire burning when I second-guessed myself.*

Table of Contents

About the Author

 **Iris Classon** is a force of nature. Her unique and engaging methods of teaching complex topics have garnered her considerable respect from the developer community and a great deal of media attention – Channel 9, Hanselminutes, Computer Sweden, and Developer Magazine – just to name a few. She is a Microsoft MVP and holds multiple certifications. Currently a freelance developer with her company, In Love With Code LTD, Iris can be found consulting for large enterprises and working on backend systems and operations for startups. She often speaks at conferences such as TechDays and NDC and at user groups. Her passion for teaching code extends to her tweets @IrisClasson, her popular blog, StackOverflow, MSDN, and a myriad of other social media sites.

About the Technical Reviewer

 **Sean Whitesell** is a software developer in Tulsa, Oklahoma, and has been the president of the Tulsa .NET User Group since 2009. He is a frequent speaker at user groups and conferences. Sean has more than 18 years of experience in various aspects of software development ranging from Azure, Kubernetes, client-server, ASP.NET, Angular, embedded, and electronics development. His passions are in solving problems programmatically, coding craftsmanship, and teaching programming and martial arts.

About the Technical Reviewer

Acknowledgments

I have to start by thanking my editors Jill Balzano and Joan Murray for their patience and support in writing this book. I had an exciting year with a move, travelling, belly growing, and childbirth, and Joan and Jill gave me flexibility when I needed it, focus and guidance when required, and most importantly, helped me stay on track so I could deliver this book.

My place of work, Konstrukt, has been vital for this book – not only by trusting me with publishing vital parts of our code but also by letting me share our journey.

But as cheesy as it might sound, the biggest thank you goes to my partner Emanuel Olsson. Dealing with a stressed programmer is one thing, but a pregnant and stressed programmer is a whole new ball game! Whenever I felt my motivation and energy drop, I could always turn to him for support.

Lastly, I want to thank my son, Loke Tiberiu, for keeping me company – kicking and rolling in my belly, burping and farting once out (and maybe a tiny bit of crying) – while writing this book. I couldn't have asked for better company!

Introduction

I remember when I was straight out of school how excited I was whenever I came across something new – a new language, framework, or tool – it was always fun and exciting to play around with it. After many years as a programmer, I still get excited, but I am also increasingly skeptical and hesitant to invest time in new things as I've seen so many come and go and not survive the test of time. This also goes for migrating existing systems. I used to want to rewrite everything, and I probably still do, but I've also seen how expensive this can get without necessarily yielding a better code base or system.

When .NET Core was first announced, I was enthusiastic but skeptical – even a bit cynical. I had jumped on the portable class library train early on and had my share of fun with that, and therefore the promise of .NET Core wasn't something I was going to believe until I could see it delivered. ASP.NET Core was the first framework to make use of .NET Core, and although I could see many benefits early on (often a result of getting to rewrite something that has collected technical debt over time), I wanted to wait and see where this would go. As the adoption rate increased, along with the contribution rate to this open source framework, we started discussing at work if ASP.NET Core could be something for us. The problems I came across while trying to answer that question were that information on ASP.NET Core was lacking, was referring to older versions, was scattered, inconsistent, and most importantly lacked real-world examples of doing large-scale migrations. If you, like me, are a natural skeptic, I can imagine that you would lean more toward a no in terms of migrating, even more so if you get lost in the information and opinion jungle, we spend most our time in. My aim with this book is to foremost show a real-world example, with actual code from our system, of a migration from ASP.NET to ASP.NET Core neatly organized in easy-to-follow steps. While the book won't be an authoritative guide on ASP.NET Core (there are plenty of excellent books that cover ASP.NET Core), it will cover what you need to know to make a decision on whether or not to migrate. It will cover your migration options, how to do an analysis, and prepare, migrate, and maintain your web services. The book also has an extensive list of resources and tools that can come in handy, as well as plenty of examples of both problems and solutions that you might come across. This book has all the information that I was struggling to find, and my hope is that this book will answer the majority of your questions and let you focus on building awesome software be that with ASP.NET Core or not.

A Bit of Background Material

When I first wrote the outline for this book, I didn't plan on spending too much time explaining ASP.NET Core. I would assume a certain level of understanding from you, the reader, and we'd hit the ground running. But, often as developers, we are pressed for time and decisions are made when we start implementing, with good intentions to at some point take the time to dive deep in a new technology, but as we all can attest, sometimes we never get around to it. Therefore, I want to take a little of your time in the beginning of this book to share my insights and cover some of the more valuable aspects of ASP.NET Core that you might not be aware of. Hopefully, this will allow us to create a solid base for the migration that lies ahead of us in this book.

Besides understanding .NET Core, .NET Standard, as well as ASP.NET Core, I also want you to have an insight into the history behind the Microsoft web development stack and how we ended up with ASP.NET Core. And an important part of that is covering the difference between ASP.

NET Web Forms, ASP.NET Web API, and ASP.NET Core. Not to mention the difference between the two project types: ASP.NET Core (.NET Core) and ASP.NET Core (.NET Framework).

Web Development Stack Timeline

Let's see if I can condense the history of ASP.NET Core and how we got here. If you have been around for a while, you know it's a long story that can be tracked back to when Classic ASP (Active Server Pages) was a thing, and maybe even further back to one of Microsoft's first inter-process communication methods, DDE (Dynamic Data Exchange), in the late 1980s. Classic ASP was a revolutionizing way of dynamically rendering server-side pages with baked-in logic, and later evolved to ASP 1.0, followed by ASP.NET and Web Forms in 2001. In 2009, ASP.NET MVC was released as a (much-needed) alternative to Web Forms. Simultaneously, communication methods evolved from DDE to DCOM, to .NET Remoting, to ASP Web Services in early 2000. In 2006, WCF (Windows Communication Foundation) was released, tying together the different options and supporting a variety of communication standards. WCF was intended to be a unified programming model for building service-oriented applications that had explicit support for service-oriented development. However, WCF had some limitations in regard to REST (Representational State Transfer) support. The WCF Web API project was intended to fill the gaps and eventually evolved and became what we today know as Web API. Web API was quickly embraced, partly because it tied in nicely with the ASP.NET MVC style of programming. Not so surprisingly, when ASP.NET Core was written, as a rewrite of ASP.NET, the two were combined (Web API and MVC). But how exactly do .NET Core, .NET Standard, and ASP.NET Core fit in?

Core and More

As I see it, there were two major driving forces that led to what we today know as .NET Core. Firstly, there was an increasing need for cross-platform compatibility to stay relevant, and secondly, we had gotten to a place where we had too many subsets of the .NET Framework, which was causing all sorts of problems as the subsets were created and maintained by different teams. 2014 was the year many exciting announcements were made by Microsoft. ASP.NET vNext was announced in April, and .NET Core in November the same year. .NET Core was a fork and open source rewrite of .NET, and likewise ASP.NET vNext was a complete rewrite of ASP.NET. It was later known as ASP.NET 5 (and by some as project K), until Microsoft realized the name was confusing and renamed it to ASP.NET Core.

In 2016, the .NET Standard was introduced to us, as a way to bring everything together. .NET Standard is a specification; it defines a set of available .NET APIs. You can think of it as interfaces and the frameworks that support the (or version of) .NET Standard as implementations. If you ever had the pleasure of working with Portable Class Libraries (PCL) and the framework union model they used, you'll be pleased to hear that .NET Standard will replace PCLs.

To sum up, ASP.NET Core is the next step in the web development evolution, an evolution that goes back more than 30 years. During that time a lot has happened; tools and frameworks have been developed and matured. The goal has always been to make it easier for us as developers to create performant, flexible, yet sturdy services that allow freedom in terms of how we communicate over the network and serve our content. ASP.NET Core puts together some of the last missing pieces in terms of combining the power of other frameworks while giving us the flexibility to choose the operating system best suited for our service and optimal performance all while encouraging best practices. You might not decide to migrate after reading this book or doing the suggested analysis, but the information will be valuable nonetheless as ASP.NET Core is the future of web development with the Microsoft stack.

CHAPTER 1

The SaaS System in Question

I never pictured myself working at a startup. For as long as I've been working as a developer, it has mostly been consulting gigs, and to me a startup meant unreasonable working hours, low pay, a bunch of hipsters arguing over what toys and games to stock in the conference room, plus little to no stability. But, never say never, especially in the tech world.

One evening, I joined a friend of mine for a late-night coding session with his business partner Johan (also a developer). They were battling performance problems and bugs into the wee hours of the morning. One evening turned into several weekends in a row, complete with the pick and mix candy (a Swedish specialty), more caffeine than anyone should consume, and raucous music pouring out from the speakers. We coded tirelessly in that office overlooking the city center, and I ended up offering to help profile the services they were experiencing problems with. The services were ASP.NET services with significant performance and memory use problems. At that time, the answer to the problem was to create a local, on-prem solution for each customer. Each customer had a local installation, not a big deal, as there were only two customers. But, understanding that their client list was growing, I think we all recognized the value of taking the system to the cloud to make a multitenant solution. The partners chose Azure, an excellent choice I thought, as I had a decent amount of experience with Azure and had been impressed. Then the

© Iris Classon 2019
I. Classon, *Migrating ASP.NET Microservices to ASP.NET Core*,
https://doi.org/10.1007/978-1-4842-4327-5_1

elephant entered the room, how do we make the shift from on-prem to multitenant? Doesn't this mean a lot of rewriting and reworking of code? What about all the features and bug fixes we had promised our current and prospective clients? I could see this was daunting to all involved, but I also recognized it as a great opportunity. In no time, I found myself working full days with complete access and rights to all their Azure accounts and servers. Long story short, I signed a contract and was now officially part of a startup.

You might be wondering why I'm telling you all this. The backstory ends at the point when we started migrating, a great starting point to share with you my experience, advice, shortcuts, and hard-earned lessons. So, let's get started.

We will begin our journey by learning what the system does, its parts, and how it all comes together. Throughout this book, I will use a ton of example code. I want to keep everything as authentic as possible, and therefore the services and code you will see will be actual working code from our system (with minor modifications to protect the innocent) and yes, the good, the bad, and the ugly. My goal is to provide you with a realistic scenario to work from, and something transferable and relevant to what you are working on.

Installation Requirements

Although you can run ASP.NET Core on Linux and use, for example, Visual Studio Code as your editor, I've chosen to use Visual Studio Community Edition (free) on Windows to leverage some additional tools and extensions that will simplify the migration. These tools only simplify the migration, and the vital steps of the migration are not dependent upon the tools, and alternative ways will be covered in this book.

Requirements for a migration using the steps described in the book:

- Windows 10

- Visual Studio Community Edition 2017 (free)

- .NET Core SDK (latest or the version you are targeting)

Additional requirements for running the examples in the book:

- IIS 7 or later

- Git and Git Bash

- SQL Server Express 2016

Multitenant Software as a Service (SaaS)

The system itself is, as I mentioned, a multitenant solution. It's a SaaS system (Software as a Service), which means it has a cloud computing service model where the system is centrally hosted. The clients, whom we refer to as tenants, do not have to manage or control the infrastructure. That is unless they choose, or rather insist on, an on-premise installation (we have some government institutions that for legal reasons cannot use the cloud solution). The tenants are merely consumers of the applications, and while it feels like they have each their own dedicated cloud installation of our system, they are using the same applications and services. We get the benefit of not having to manage x-number of infrastructure setups and discuss hardware and software requirements and licenses, support becomes more manageable, and we can roll out patches and updates as we please. There is also a significant financial gain to this, which is another important factor. But, the challenges are plenty. Data security is an obvious challenge, and so is uptime. We have SLAs (Service Level Agreements) toward our tenants, but we also have SLAs with our cloud vendor and the services we use there. One of our biggest challenges, and a very common one for SaaS solutions, is load, latency, and performance. Load is uncertain and very difficult to predict. And the performance issues we were seeing in the on-premise implementations significantly increased when we adopted the cloud model. Why? We work with data, a lot of it.

What the System Does

Konstrukt is a planning platform designed to handle different types of planning scenarios for all kind of organizations.

Any quantitative planning and data consolidation, simple or complex, can be managed in a secure and user-friendly way, replacing the misuse of Excel in many organizations. The system is flexible and covers a wide range of planning scenarios such as strategic planning, rolling forecasting, data-driven budgeting, workforce capacity planning, compensation and equity planning, and so on. It probably doesn't come as a surprise that the system has a great deal of complexity, and a reoccurring challenge we have is performance. I'll get back to this in the next chapter where we discuss the pros and cons of doing a migration.

Architecture

Konstrukt consists of nine ASP.NET Web API services and one stateless and decoupled client written in JavaScript, HTML, and CSS (Figure 1-1). Each tenant has their own database, and we currently only use SQL Server for our databases. The majority of the services share the same databases on the same server cluster, some separated by schemas, and we also have NoSQL databases (MongoDB) used by some services. Deceptively this makes it look like we have a true microservice architecture, but we don't. We have a mix of microservices and what I often refer to as a distributed monolith. A distributed monolith is a system deployed as several small services that resemble microservices that are fairly well scoped and small, but rely on the same datastore and are not failure resistant. Some developers still refer to services like these as microservices, while some would disagree. While the title of the book talks about migrating microservices, we will migrate services with various degrees of decoupling and failure resistance to give you a realistic picture of how it is to migrate an existing complex system, legacy or not. If you have a monolith, in other words, a single-tier application, don't worry. Some of our services are more or less monoliths, and I'll make sure to cover migration examples including those.

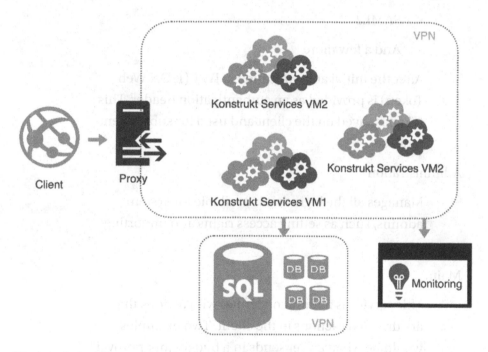

Figure 1-1. *The system we are migrating*

I'm only going to use some services as an example for the migration, but in case you wonder how the system looks like, these are the main services and what they do:

Authentication

> Manages authentication. We support several authentication methods, such as

> - Internal database login
> - ADFS
> - SAML2
> - And a few more

> After the initial authentication, a JWT (JSON Web Token) is provided as an authentication header. This token is saved on the client and used for subsequent requests.

Administration

> Manages all the logic that is available for system admins, such as setting access rights and importing users.

Main

> This service is mainly concerned with actions that are driven by actions in the client. Two examples would be when a user sends in a budget for approval and when a user adds a comment on a budget.

AggregationEngine

> Writes and reads budget data to the user budget line tables.

CalculationEngine

> Queues and processes calculations that generate data for the different plans and budgets.

NotificationService

> Manages notifications, currently WebSocket notifications. Notifications can be messages in the chat or user notifications when a budget has been submitted for approval. We use SignalR for our notifications, a popular library for working with real-time web communication.

Example System Used in This Book

As you probably have concluded, the system is of considerable size. It's not colossal, but large nonetheless. For the purpose of this book, I've trimmed the solution, and I have some particular services in mind that will receive more attention in this book as shown in Figure 1-2.

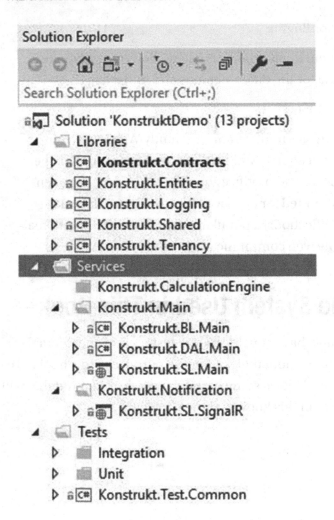

Figure 1-2. *The trimmed down version of Konstrukt that I'm using as an example in this book*

This book focuses on migrating the Konstrukt.SL.Main service and its dependencies (shown in Figure 1-3) while making sure that the solution libraries it depends on can also be used by services that are not migrated. This means that while the service will target .NET Core, it's solution dependencies will be migrated to .NET Standard. Konstrukt.SL.Main was the starting point for Konstrukt and has subsequently accumulated a fair bit of spaghetti code over the years. As we are moving toward a microservice architecture, we have broken out areas of responsibilities to separate services, and Konstrukt.SL.Main was an excellent candidate for that. I'll get back to this later in the book.

I also want to mention the notification service, which at the moment manages WebSocket notifications using SignalR. This is a lightweight service with just a few dependencies that are popular libraries – which makes it a good candidate for a full migration. However, Asp.NET Core SignalR differs significantly from SignalR, and a migration would require a separate book on the topic, and therefore I've omitted the code for the service.

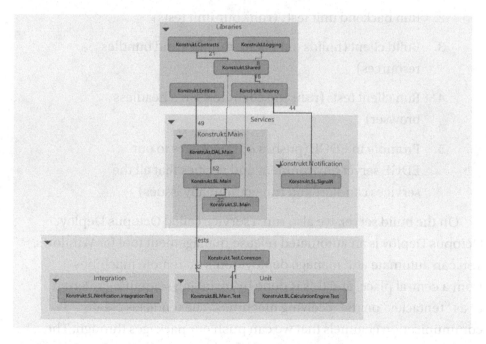

Figure 1-3. *The dependency graph for the example code*

Pipeline

Later in the book we will also take a look at how we have to modify the pipeline as we migrate our services and libraries. Our current pipeline looks like this.

We use Git as our version control system, and we use GitHub for our repository. We have a build server that runs TeamCity – TeamCity is a build server service. It runs the following build steps sequentially – and if one step fails, the other steps won't run:

1.   Build backend (builds the backend code, and packages each service as a NuGet package)

2.   Run backend unit tests (runs our unit tests)

3.   Build client (builds our client, minifies and bundles resources)

4.   Run client tests (runs the client tests in a headless browser)

5.   Promote to EDGE (pushes our packages to our EDGE server environment and verifies that all the services can start and run without any issues)

On the build server, we also run a service called Octopus Deploy. Octopus Deploy is an automated release management tool for Windows. You can automate and manage deployments on remote machines from a central place, and this is done by installing something referred to as "tentacles" on the receiving machines. The tentacles create communication channels that we can push our packages through. The machines are organized in groups tagged as an environment. We have different number of machines depending on the environment. Our EDGE environment is just one virtual machine, because we only want to have a first place to deploy to and make sure everything runs fine. Our second environment is our QA (quality assurance) environment. This is where we do our testing, and we have the services spread out on two machines. Our AT environment (acceptance testing) has four machines and is identical to the production environment as it is the final stop before deploying to production. Acceptance testing is the final testing that we do, and we have both certain customers and implementation consultants (consultants that help the tenant configure their data and calculations) testing in AT. The final environment, also with four virtual machines, is PROD – production. Ideally, we would have each service run on a single virtual machine so we would have proper isolation, but unfortunately that would be too expensive for us. That is also one of the reasons that we would like to migrate our services, and I'm going to talk about that a whole lot more in the next chapter.

Summary

In this chapter we've taken a look at the Konstrukt architecture and what the system does. The system consists of nine services, various tools, and a SQL server for storage. Konstrukt does numeric planning for enterprises and manages performance-sensitive operations tied to the planning and data consolidation. Throughout the book we will use a slice of the system to guide you through a step-by-step migration, including changes to the deployment pipeline.

In the next chapter, we will discuss the pros and cons of migrating.

CHAPTER 2

Should We Migrate?

This is by far the most popular question I get when I tell people about our migration or when I do a conference session on the topic. There is no straightforward answer, as most decisions in tech – it depends.

We were in Hungary for a weeklong kickoff with work when we first started discussing migrating to .NET Core. The kickoff was a yearly tradition where we set aside a whole week to learn new things without the pressure of having to reply to customers, deliver new features, or do other typical work. .NET Core was new and sexy, and it had come up in conversation several times.

I had a new colleague, Tobias, and he had gone through our solution and removed all the assemblies we weren't using*. Furthermore, we decided to see if we could migrate to .NET Core without too much trouble. We spent the week looking into that, as well as discussing the pros and cons. Knowing the general pros and cons might give you a quick idea if there is something to gain from a migration. Here is an overview of the pros and cons.

---

* ReSharper, a commercial Visual Studio extension, has a feature that lets you discover and remove unused assemblies. There is also a free extension, ResolveUR, that does the same. Take your time, remove one at the time, and don't forget to test in between. We will look at this in a later chapter.

© Iris Classon 2019
I. Classon, *Migrating ASP.NET Microservices to ASP.NET Core*,
https://doi.org/10.1007/978-1-4842-4327-5_2

The Benefits

Here is an overview of what many consider as main benefits of migrating – or improvements to ASP.NET Core. Some of these vary depending on the version of ASP.NET Core, and some also depend on whether or not you are targeting .NET Core (compared to targeting the full .NET Framework). The items are not listed in order of importance.

Performance

The expected performance gains would be very important for us as we have a system that does heavy work, a lot of calculations, and would also need to be able to handle many concurrent requests. Performance in ASP.NET Core has improved in many ways (Figures 2-1 and 2-2) – the library itself has been improved during the rewrite, and so has the .NET Core framework. Additionally, other big changes such as modularity and independent hosting have also contributed to improved performance.

ASP.NET Core is between 6 and 23 times faster than ASP.NET, faster than Node.js, and could by the second version handle over 1.5 million requests per second. In ASP.NET Core 2.2 the performance has improved further. If you want to learn more about the benchmarking, visit the repository at `https://github.com/aspnet/benchmarks`.

Rnk	Framework	Best performance (higher is better)		Cls	Lng	Plt	FE	Aos	IA	E
1	aspcore	6,970,937	100.0% (99.0%)	Plt	C#	.NE	kes	Lin	Rea	
2	aspcore-mw	2,969,533	42.6% (42.2%)	Mcr	C#	.NE	kes	Lin	Rea	
3	aspcore-mvc	1,032,068	14.8% (14.7%)	Ful	C#	.NE	kes	Lin	Rea	
4	aspcore-mono	880,263	12.6% (12.5%)	Plt	C#	.NE	kes	Lin	Rea	
5	nodejs	826,111	11.9% (11.7%)	Plt	JS	njs	Non	Lin	Rea	
6	aspcore-mono-mw	461,127	6.6% (6.5%)	Mcr	C#	.NE	kes	Lin	Rea	
7	aspcore-mono-mvc	281,549	4.0% (4.0%)	Ful	C#	.NE	kes	Lin	Rea	1
8	nancy-netcore	215,608	3.1% (3.1%)	Mcr	C#	.NE	kes	Lin	Rea	
9	nancy-mono	8,394	0.1% (0.1%)	Mcr	C#	.NE	kes	Lin	Rea	
10	aspnet-mono-ngx	5,513	0.1% (0.1%)	Plt	C#	.NE	ngx	Lin	Rea	
11	sailsjs	0	0.0% (0.0%)	Ful	JS	njs	Non	Lin	Rea	

Best plaintext responses per second, Dell R440 Xeon Gold + 10 GbE (11 tests)

Figure 2-1. *Benchmarking results for plain text responses per second for ASP.NET Core, Node.js and ASP.NET Mono*

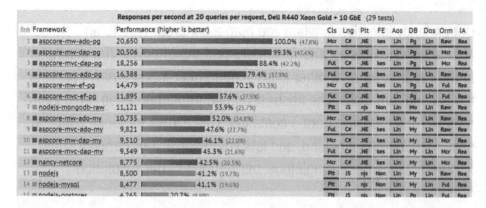

Rnk	Framework	Performance (higher is better)	Cls	Lng	Plt	FE	Aos	DB	Dos	Orm	IA
		Responses per second at 20 queries per request, Dell R440 Xeon Gold + 10 GbE (29 tests)									
1	aspcore-mw-ado-pg	20,650 100.0% (47.8%)	Mcr	C#	.NE	kes	Lin	Pg	Lin	Raw	Rea
2	aspcore-mw-dap-pg	20,506 99.3% (47.4%)	Mcr	C#	.NE	kes	Lin	Pg	Lin	Mcr	Rea
3	aspcore-mvc-dap-pg	18,256 88.4% (42.2%)	Ful	C#	.NE	kes	Lin	Pg	Lin	Mcr	Rea
4	aspcore-mvc-ado-pg	16,388 79.4% (37.9%)	Ful	C#	.NE	kes	Lin	Pg	Lin	Raw	Rea
5	aspcore-mw-ef-pg	14,479 70.1% (33.5%)	Mcr	C#	.NE	kes	Lin	Pg	Lin	Ful	Rea
6	aspcore-mvc-ef-pg	11,895 57.6% (27.5%)	Ful	C#	.NE	kes	Lin	Pg	Lin	Ful	Rea
7	nodejs-mongodb-raw	11,121 53.9% (25.7%)	Plt	JS	njs	Non	Lin	Mo	Lin	Raw	Rea
8	aspcore-mw-ado-my	10,735 52.0% (24.8%)	Mcr	C#	.NE	kes	Lin	My	Lin	Raw	Rea
9	aspcore-mvc-ado-my	9,821 47.6% (22.7%)	Ful	C#	.NE	kes	Lin	My	Lin	Raw	Rea
10	aspcore-mw-dap-my	9,510 46.1% (22.0%)	Mcr	C#	.NE	kes	Lin	My	Lin	Mcr	Rea
11	aspcore-mvc-dap-my	9,349 45.3% (21.6%)	Ful	C#	.NE	kes	Lin	My	Lin	Mcr	Rea
12	nancy-netcore	8,775 42.5% (20.3%)	Mcr	C#	.NE	kes	Lin	My	Lin	Mcr	Rea
13	nodejs	8,500 41.2% (19.7%)	Plt	JS	njs	Non	Lin	My	Lin	Raw	Rea
14	nodejs-mysql	8,477 41.1% (19.6%)	Plt	JS	njs	Non	Lin	My	Lin	Ful	Rea
15	nodejs-postgres	4,265 20.7% (9.9%)	Plt	JS	njs	Non	Lin	Pg	Lin	Ful	Rea

Figure 2-2. *Benchmarking results for responses per second at 20 queries per request for ASP.NET Core, Node.js and ASP.NET Mono*

Built-In Dependency Injection and Logging

As with any rewrite, the Microsoft team, together with the community, set out to write a much better version and to encourage good practices right from the start. Two noticeable new improvements are built-in dependency injection (DI) and logging. If you already make heavy use of dependency injection, this might not be a big deal – but ASP.NET Core lets you easily plug in your preferred container resolver, and from there on everything just works. Integrating DI in a library is not revolutionary, but what is a noticeable difference from before is how the DI now naturally blends in with ASP.NET Core. For example, reading and working with configuration files also use DI, and you can map a settings section to a concrete class of the abstract type IOptions<MySettings> and work with strongly typed accessors to your settings. We already had set up our own version of this, but this certainly makes everything cleaner.

ASP.NET Core encourages better practices – and with better practices you can expect more pliable code that is easier to test and maintain. If you have a system that undergoes a lot of changes you've experienced locking yourself in on bad solutions, this might be an important benefit.

Dependency injection is when you map a concrete type to an abstraction such as an interface and inject the interface (for example) in the constructor of another class instead of creating a new concrete instance in that class. The abstraction and implementation are usually mapped and resolved from a container. This allows for loose coupling, easier testing and mocking, and lets you resolve your dependencies in different ways – as singletons, per request or per resolution.

Flexible Deployment

By flexible deployment I'm referring to the fact that you can choose HTTP server, and you can choose deployment mode – self-contained or framework dependent.

By default, ASP.NET Core ships with two server implementations, Kestrel (cross-platform) and HTTP.sys (Windows), but you could use another web server as long as it is compatible. A reverse proxy server is still recommended, for example, IIS, NGINX, or Apache. Not being tied to a specific web server allows us to be flexible and is also in part what lets us deploy to different operating systems. ASP.NET was heavily tied to IIS which made portability impossible. It also had heavy dependencies that would be pulled in regardless of them being used or not, with slow request pipelines that had unnecessary hurdles. OWIN, Open Web Interface for .NET, is a specification that aims to decouple the web server from the web application, and project Katana in ASP.NET (now retired) was an OWIN implementation by Microsoft. ASP.NET Core took over and fully complies with the OWIN specification. If you want to build a custom web server, you can as ASP.NET Core fully supports OWIN. If you think about it, ASP.NET Core applications are just .NET Core applications that process incoming HTTP requests.

Let's talk more about deployment. When you deploy you can choose to deploy the application or service as self-contained application – this means all the DLLs it needs are packaged with it and you are not dependent on a system-wide installation of the libraries (pertaining to ASP.NET Core and .NET Core) the application is dependent on. The finished package is larger, but you have everything you need and this can simplify deployment – in particular, when you want to just zip everything up and have it work on any machine. The downside is that you become responsible for managing the version, and you need to think about the target framework or frameworks before you publish and pack. The other option is the one that we are more familiar with from ASP.NET, framework-dependent deployment. The libraries have to be installed system wide; in other words, the system you deploy to has to be prepared and maintained. I'll get back to this later as there are some caveats with both options. The important takeaway is that you have options that you don't have with ASP.NET, options that let you tweak and customize the deployment to better suit your scenario and requirements.

Modular

One thing I didn't mention in the preceding section is the modular HTTP request pipeline, a result of implementing the OWIN specification. This is available in ASP.NET with Katana, but comes more naturally in ASP.NET Core. To explain this in simple terms, you can very easily plug in your own middleware that interacts with the requests and responses on their way in and out. We use this to modify our requests, custom logging, and a few more things. It lets us return or redirect early in the request processing. This modularity is a theme that you see throughout ASP.NET Core. For example, everything is a NuGet package. You don't add references, you add NuGet packages. And there are many packages, because the big ASP.NET Framework has been completely rewritten in ASP.NET Core to consist of many smaller libraries. The upside is that Microsoft can release more often, the downside is of course version alignment and dependencies. This has been sorted with metapackages, a package that references other packages. It includes all supported packages by the ASP.NET Core team and the Entity Framework team. We'll talk more about this later.

Open Source and Community Driven

I mentioned earlier that ASP.NET Core is open source, and this is fantastic.
There are many good things that come with that, and transparency is the
biggest one I would say. I can see the roadmap and join in on the discussion if
I want to; I can see issues and breaking changes, suggestions, and discussions.
And an active community is doing the same and keeps pushing the projects
forward all while making sure that best practices are followed and possible
future issues are considered. There are currently over 147 repositories
(including Entity Framework Core repositories) and growing! (Figure 2-3).

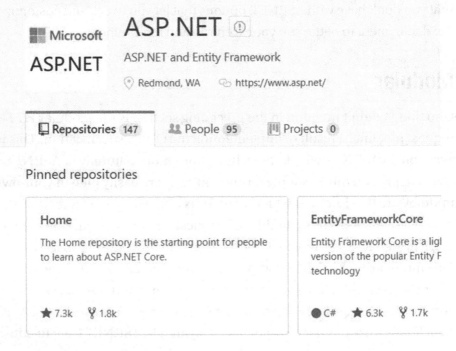

Figure 2-3. *The ASP.NET GitHub page*

You can contribute, and it's easier than you think! For example, I've
submitted issues, joined the discussions, and helped other developers
with workarounds. The access to the code means that debugging is much

easier, and you can familiarize yourself with the code and see the history of the code. Very useful when classes suddenly disappear or an issue is solved and you want to know how. Of course, you can decompile any library in .NET, but there might be legal limitations depending on the user agreement and your country of residence. Regardless, you wouldn't have the history and the issues and discussions tied to a particular line of code.

Perfect for Containers

By nature, .NET Core is lightweight and modular, which makes it much easier to use with containers. Container is the concept of virtualization at the operating system level. From the inside of a container, it is a self-contained machine. It thinks it has its own operating system and everything that comes with it. For the services running inside the container (virtual boundaries), it feels like they run on a dedicated machine. In reality, they share the same machine as other containers using the same host and can only access resources within the container or explicitly made available. It feels like a virtual machine, but you don't have the overhead of a guest operating system, startup time, and more. The operating system is reused, and instead virtual boundaries let us work with containers as if they were separate machines. You basically bundle your application with everything it needs, and you get consistency, portability, flexibility, testability, and isolation in one package.

Containers have been around for a long time in the Linux world, but security and isolation concerns impeded the container movement on Windows. Thankfully we have seen massive changes the last few years, and now containers are first-class citizen even on Windows and in Visual Studio. As a matter of fact, you can run your applications in containers straight from the IDE. It's either just a checkbox you need to tick when you create a new project or you can add that functionality to an existing project. Visual Studio will create the container files (called Docker files) as well as Compose files – files that use Docker Compose to run several containers that can communicate with each other.

Server applications that run in the background are a good fit for containers, and ASP.NET Core applications are great candidates as they are lightweight, a good "cultural fit." Let's cover some other benefits.

Cross-Platform

.NET Core can also run in a Linux environment – and that also goes for ASP.NET Core targeting the .NET Core framework. That means we can have lighter containers – and also a host that doesn't necessarily require a license. As a result, we can increase the concurrent services density. Moreover, this allows us to expand our isolated testing environment to several environments such as Quality Assurance (QA) and Acceptance Testing (AT) without the cost or hardware overhead. However, if you can't target the .NET Core framework and you have some services that have to target the full .NET Framework, you can still benefit from both containers and the cross-platform ability. Something called "hybrid swarm" (a swarm is a cluster of containers) lets us run mixed environment containers – in other words, we can run Windows and Linux applications in one cluster.

A s a startup, cost has been an issue for us straight from the start and also been something that has hindered our deployment pipeline as we have crammed several services on one machine to save money. With better isolation comes easier scaling, debugging, and deploying.

Besides these, there are also other benefits to running on other platforms – and for us that is the access to mature and well-maintained tools. While most Linux tools have a Windows equivalent, there are still some tools that have a higher maturity level on Linux that we would love to leverage.

If you want to learn more about the tools available to you on the Linux platform to manage multiple services, I would highly recommend one of my favorite books on the topic, *DevOps 2.0*.

The Challenges

Now that we have covered the main selling points, it's important that we also take a look at the downsides so we can take these into account when we make our decisions.

Lack of Resources and Documentation

Many of the downsides to ASP.NET Core has to do with the lack of maturity compared to ASP.NET. There is less help available online when it comes to forums, articles, and documentation. If we compare questions asked on StackOverflow with the ASP.NET Core tag vs. the ASP.NET tag, we see a significant difference. ASP.NET has had the time to collect resources and has been adopted by many developers (Figure 2-4).

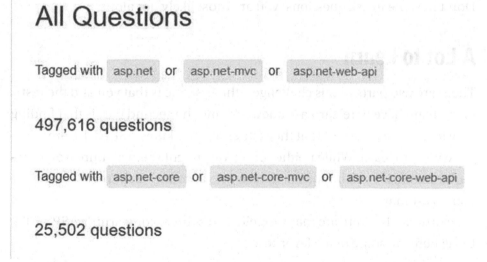

Figure 2-4. *Questions asked with the ASP.NET Core vs. ASP.NET tags on StackOverflow at the time of writing*

This will change over time, and it's worth keeping in mind that it can also be a challenge to sort through the many different ways of solving ASP.NET-related problems as that framework also changed over time. Nonetheless, one of the biggest downsides of migrating to ASP.NET Core is that there are less resources available although ASP.NET Core is catching up. Knowing where to look helps, and the top five places I would recommend are

- Documentation

- GitHub repository

- Microsoft blogs

- Forums such as MSDN and StackOverflow

- Developer blogs such as those by Microsoft MVPs

You can also reach out to the team on social media such as Twitter and support forums and by submitting or commenting on issues on GitHub. Don't hesitate to ask questions; you are most likely not alone.

A Lot to Learn

There are two parts to this challenge – the first one is that you and the rest of the team have to relearn a framework, and the second part is that finding new teammates requires that they either already know ASP.NET Core or are willing to learn. While neither of the two might seem an unreasonable requirement, it's still important to take into account – in particular when you do estimates.

Fortunately, there are many excellent resources for learning ASP.NET Core; here are some of my favorites:

- ASP.NET Core documentation has very good articles on how to get started as well as solving particular problems. Start by looking there as the documentation is maintained by the community and is kept up to date.

- Apress has several books you can choose from. Make sure you get the latest edition and for the right ASP.NET Core version.

- Microsoft Virtual Academy offers free training with hands-on examples, and you might also be able to find some free books by Microsoft press.

- Online video learning by, for example, Pluralsight. The majority of these sites have free trials. There are also YouTube videos, but they don't go through the same review process. You can also find videos from conferences that are free to watch and download.

- Channel 9 hosts videos from Microsoft conferences such as BUILD (conference where changes and new products are announced) as well as Microsoft produced educational videos and recorded streams by the ASP. NET Core team.

- Other large conferences such as NDC and .NET Conf also publish their conference recordings for free.

Versions and Changes

While Microsoft together with the community is trying their best to avoid breaking changes, there will always be some – in particular in the beginning. The first few versions of ASP.NET Core had several unpopular breaking changes, such as going back to csproj project format instead of using JSON.

Navigating between versions, information and documentation on versions can be a pain. Not to mention migrating between versions, or deploying different versions (deployment has been simplified and I'd say deploying different versions is less painful than dealing with ASP.NET version deployments if you are targeting ASP.NET Core 2.0 and up).

The reason why there are breaking changes is in large part due to the fact that ASP.NET Core was new and hadn't found its identity in the beginning. It is also open source and there is a big push from the community to implement the best possible solutions, even if that means going back on a previous decision. I recommend that keep an eye on issues tagged with breaking-changes in the ASP.NET Core repository (Figure 2-5). Additionally, always double check that you are using the right version of the documentation when browsing the documentation (Figure 2-6).

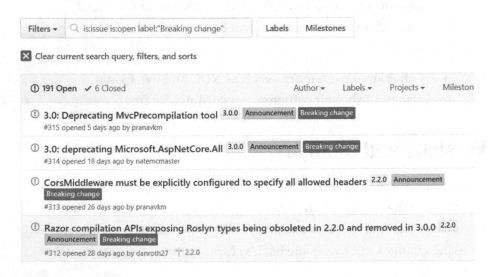

Figure 2-5. *Make sure you keep an eye on issues tagged with "Breaking change"*

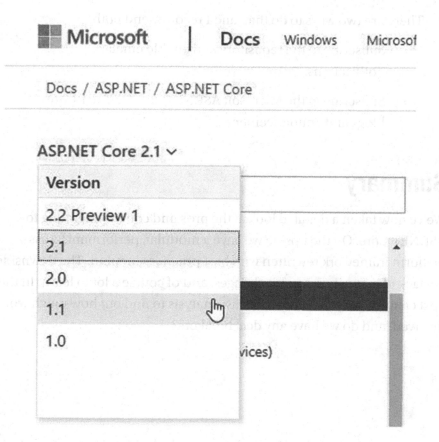

Figure 2-6. *Make sure to pick the right version when you read the documentation*

ASP.NET Core is maturing, the adoption rate is great, and the community is very engaged. This means that it has become more stable, there is more pressure to avoid breaking change, and there are less big changes as the foundation has been built.

I always recommend developers to keep an eye on the frameworks that they use – in particular the larger ones such as ASP.NET Core.

There are two ways to do that, and I recommend both:

- Subscribe to the repository and enable email notifications.

- Subscribe to the Microsoft ASP.NET and ASP.NET Core blogs and announcements.

Summary

We've now taken a detailed look at the pros and cons of migrating to ASP.NET Core. On the upside we have a modular, performant, cross-platform framework rewritten with best practices in mind. The downsides are lack of maturity, frequent changes, and of course a lot to learn. In the next chapter, we will do an extensive analysis to find out how much work is involved, and do we have any deal breakers?

CHAPTER 3

Phase 1: Analysis

It was early summer of 2016 and the team was in Hungary for a week of workshops and fun. Every year we would take a week somewhere remote and spend the days learning new, but relevant, skills and the afternoons and evenings building a good company culture and exchange knowledge. Our team had recently hired another backend developer, Tobias, and he was just as eager as me to explore .NET Core. We had spent 2 days penetration testing and had finished a security evaluation of the system. While sitting at a lovely café, we started discussing ASP.NET Core and if that was something we should consider. Naturally, we started talking about dependencies and what could be migrated – and if we had any deal breakers. I pulled up my laptop, and we started going through our packages and references one by one.

That was the start of our journey migrating to ASP.NET Core. Although we didn't do a full analysis or even attempt a migration that summer, it created a starting point. We were in the midst of moving to a new cloud provider and had our hands full with the move, but we had explored the pros and cons of migrating, and we had started analyzing our solution. Regardless of how you and your team decide to go about this, I recommend that you set aside a few days, without the pressure to produce results or joggle stories. With proper groundwork you can get a good analysis done, as well as make the migration easier.

Therefore, in this chapter, I will walk you through a deep analysis using a real-world example (that has been trimmed down for readability). We are going to prepare, analyze, and plan. Let's get started. I'm going to use the

© Iris Classon 2019
I. Classon, *Migrating ASP.NET Microservices to ASP.NET Core*,
https://doi.org/10.1007/978-1-4842-4327-5_3

Main project and its dependencies as an example in this chapter as well as briefly covering the other services at the end of the chapter.

This is how the Main service is layered (Figure 3-1):

- SL.Main: The service layer (endpoints and web service)

- BL.Main: Business logic layer

- DAL.Main: Data access layer

The projects have the following dependencies in the solution (Figure 3-2):

- "Konstrukt.Share": Contains plain objects, extensions, and utility classes

- "Konstrukt.Contracts": Interfaces used in several projects, usually defining infrastructure logic

- "Konstrukt.Tenancy": Library that makes the services multitenant. It queries a main database for tenant connection strings that are dynamically decrypted and changed per request

- "Konstrukt.Entities": The entity objects and the EF context model

- "Konstrukt.Logging": Library that manages logging to different sources

Relevant test projects:

- "Konstrukt.Main.Tests": Unit tests

- "Konstrukt.Tests.Common": Base classes, helpers, and mocks for unit tests

Integration tests are excluded for Konstrukt.Main in this example.

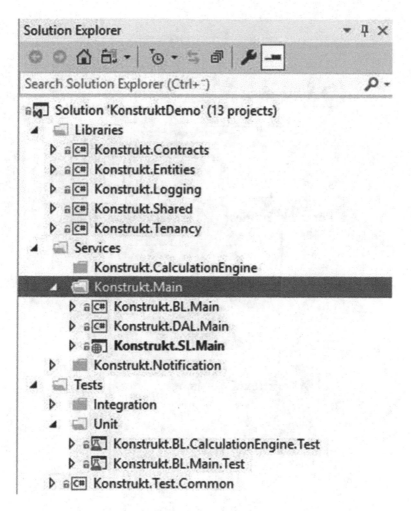

Figure 3-1. Project structure

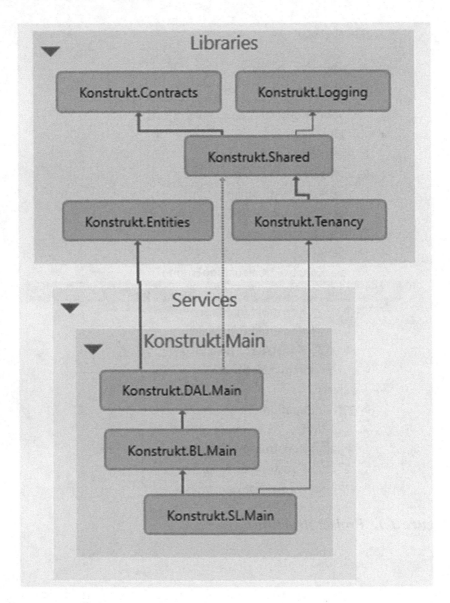

Figure 3-2. *SL.Main dependency diagram*

Preparing the Projects

When we do an analysis, we want to have as little noise as possible. We also certainly don't want to do any pointless analysis and planning for dependencies that we aren't using. Therefore, we are going to remove unused members, types, and references. But before we go ahead and do that, we will first upgrade the projects and target a newer version of the .NET Framework.

Retargeting

You might have to update Visual Studio to target a newer framework. If you don't see the framework version you want to target as an option under Properties ➤ Application ➤ Target Framework, then check for Visual Studio updates, run through them, and then bring up the Visual Studio Installer and make sure that the target framework is installed.

You can retarget by right-clicking a project node in Solution Explorer and selecting Properties. Under the Application tab, you can change the target framework as shown in Figure 3-3.

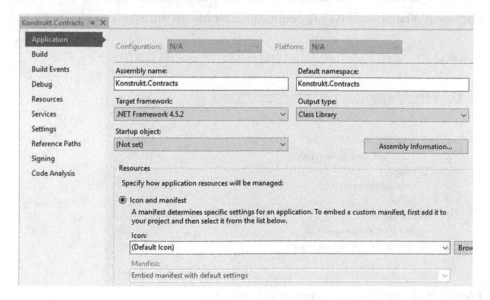

Figure 3-3. *Properties for the Konstrukt.Contracts library*

You can also do this by unloading the project and changing the TargetFrameWorkVersion in the csproj file. A tiny detail about ASP.NET Core that I like is that as with other .NET Core projects, you don't have to unload the project first to edit the project file – you can simply open it. You will also notice that the project file is much cleaner – and thus easier to work with. Changing every project can be a lot of work depending on how many you have, and I'd like to recommend an extension that you can use to retarget all in one go. I would prefer to target the latest framework version, but if that is not an option for you, then at least target 6.2.

To retarget the projects, we are going to use the Target Framework Migrator by Pavel Samokha. Close Visual Studio and download the extension from `https://marketplace.visualstudio.com/items?itemName=PavelSamokha.TargetFrameworkMigrator`.

Select the target framework, and the projects you want to retarget, and give it a few minutes. If the target framework is missing from the drop-down menu, you can add it manually to the frameworks.xml file that the extension uses. The file can be found under extensions in the user AppData/Local folder (Figure 3-4). For example, here is my path: %LocalAppData%\ Microsoft\VisualStudio\15.0_3eebc2a9\Extensions\0uwpe4cg.cv5

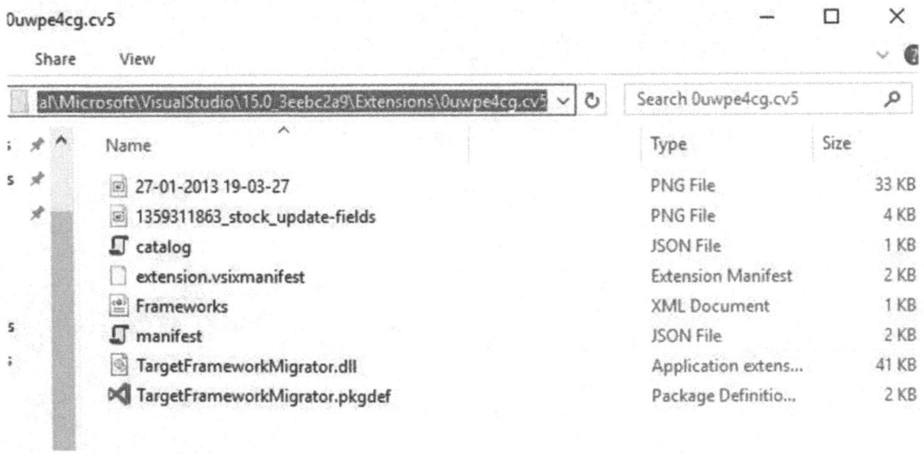

Figure 3-4. *Where the extension is located*

Modify the XML file and add the target framework as shown in Figure 3-5.

```
Frameworks.xml* ⇆ ×
 1    <?xml version="1.0" encoding="utf-8" ?>
 2  ⊟<Frameworks>
 3      <Framework Id="262663" Name=".NETFramework,Version=v4.7.2"/>
 4
 5      <Framework Id="262151" Name=".NETFramework,Version=v4.7"/>
 6      <Framework Id="262662" Name=".NETFramework,Version=v4.6.2"/>
 7      <Framework Id="262406" Name=".NETFramework,Version=v4.6.1"/>
 8      <Framework Id="262150" Name=".NETFramework,Version=v4.6"/>
 9      <Framework Id="262661" Name=".NETFramework,Version=v4.5.2"/>
10      <Framework Id="262405" Name=".NETFramework,Version=v4.5.1"/>
11      <Framework Id="262149" Name=".NETFramework,Version=v4.5"/>
12      <Framework Id="262144" Name=".NETFramework,Version=v4.0"/>
13      <Framework Id="262144" Name=".NETFramework,Version=v4.0,Profile=Client"/>
14      <Framework Id="196613" Name=".NETFramework,Version=v3.5"/>
15      <Framework Id="196613" Name=".NETFramework,Version=v3.5,Profile=Client"/>
16      <Framework Id="196608" Name=".NETFramework,Version=v3.0"/>
17      <Framework Id="131072" Name=".NETframework,Version=v2.0"/>
18    </Frameworks>
19
```

Figure 3-5. *You can add frameworks by adding the Name and Id*

Select all the projects and click Migrate. You can follow the progress as the project files are edited (Figure 3-6).

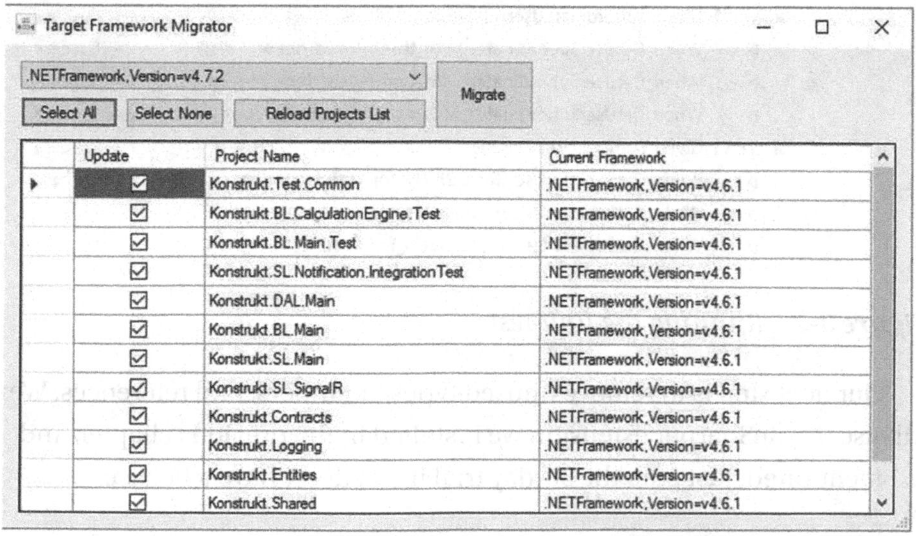

Figure 3-6. *Target Framework Migrator window in Visual Studio*

Compile and run your tests (Figure 3-7), making sure that everything compiles and runs as expected. Our unit tests use NUnit and therefore requires the NUnit Test Adapter. Due to a regression bug after a Visual Studio update, I also need to disable the following extension: Dotnet Extensions for Test Explorer. At the time of writing, this issue has been yet to be resolved, and the recommended solution is to disable Dotnet Extensions for Test Explorer. An alternative is to use the unit test runner from ReSharper – an extension we will be using for the analysis.

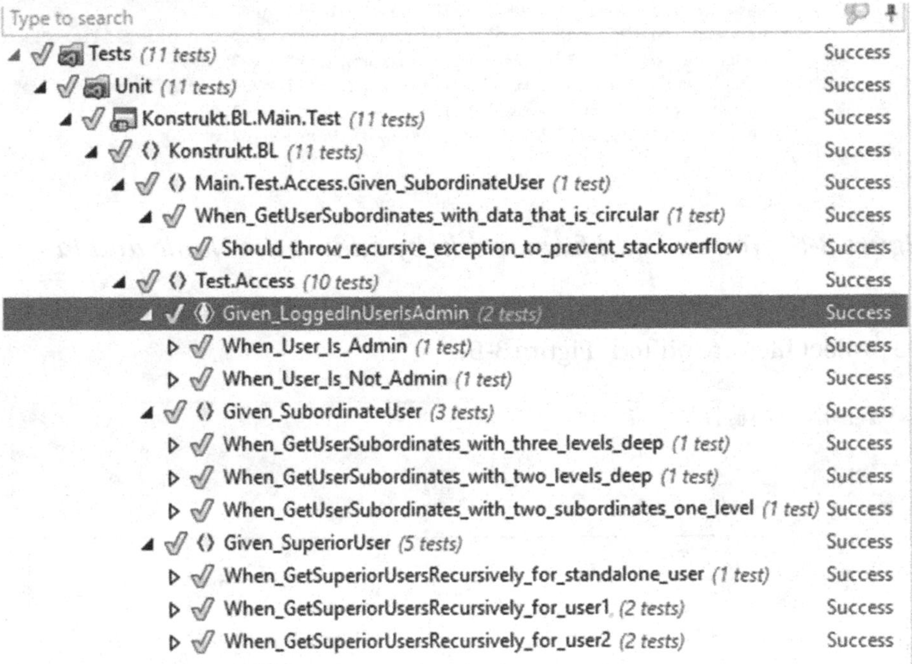

Figure 3-7. *Running the unit tests*

Our next step is to remove unused types, members, and references. We will use the ReSharper extension we installed in the previous chapter, and as I mentioned, just grab the 30-day trial if you don't have a license.

Note   Please make sure that you have created a separate branch to do the analysis if you use Git for version control, or at least use a copy of the solution. Preferably do a commit after each major step so you can undo if something goes wrong.

Removing Unused Types and Members

Technically you don't really have to do this step, but it doesn't take long and can simplify things later. This is something we should do from time to time anyway, and this is a perfect opportunity. With legacy applications and libraries over time, you often end up with types or members that aren't used, so it's worth doing a quick check first. These might in turn reference assemblies, and we want to only analyze how much work this migration is going to take based on assemblies, types, and members we are using.

Tip   There is another benefit to doing this cleanup – the maintainability index is probably going to be better, as dependencies often add complexity and problems with versions and upgrades.

If you right-click a project (or the solution) and select Analyze ➤ Calculate Code Metrics (Figure 3-8), you will get the project maintainability index as well as other indicators such as cyclomatic dependency, depth of inheritance, class coupling, and lines of code (Figure 3-9).

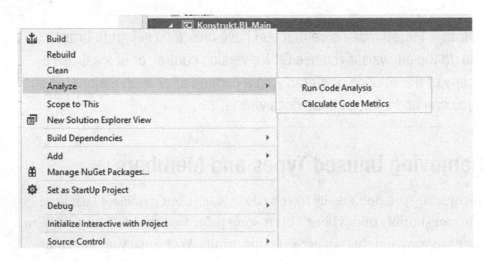

Figure 3-8. *Calculate Code Metrics can be found in the context menu for a project*

Hierarchy	Maintainability In...	Cyclomatic Com...	Depth of Inherita...	Class Coupling	Lines of Code
Services\Konstrukt.Main\Konstrukt.BL.Main (Debug)	88	85	2	64	160
▷ { } Konstrukt.BL.Main	90	4	1	8	6
▷ { } Konstrukt.BL.Main.Access	88	23	2	26	39
▷ { } Konstrukt.BL.Main.App	92	3	1	4	5
▷ { } Konstrukt.BL.Main.AppConfig	87	7	1	11	16
▷ { } Konstrukt.BL.Main.User	85	16	1	20	32
▷ { } Konstrukt.BL.Main.Util	89	32	1	25	62

Figure 3-9. *Code Metrics Results for* `Konstrukt.BL.Main`

As a fun add-on for the analysis step, why not go ahead and get the code metrics and export them to Excel. After tiding up the references, you can then run it again and compare.

Note   The maintainability index was introduced by Oman and Hagemeister in 1991. The metric is heavily criticized and there are numerous papers and articles discussing the value of the metric, many of them highlighting that other maintainability indicators are not taken into account such as naming, comments for documentation purpose, necessary complexity, how lambdas are resolved by the compiler, and other factors. This is how the maintainability index is calculated:

Maintainability Index = MAX(0,(171 - 5.2 * log(Halstead Volume) - 0.23 * (Cyclomatic Complexity) - 16.2 * log(Lines of Code))*100 / 171)

With ReSharper installed and activated, select in the main menu Resharper ➤ Inspect ➤ Code Issues in Current Project (or select solution if your solution is smaller) (Figure 3-10).

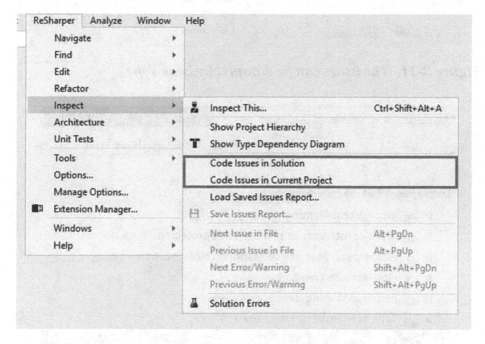

Figure 3-10. *Code Issues can be found in the ReSharper menu*

Group by Issue Type, and scroll down to "Type or member is never used" as shown in Figure 3-11. Figure 3-12 shows the result with the filter applied.

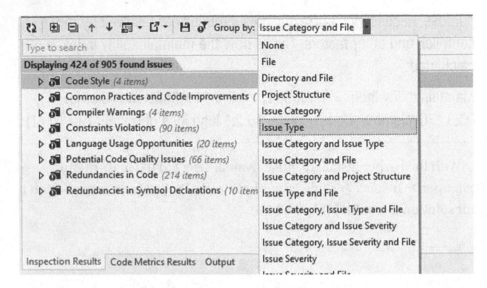

Figure 3-11. *The issues can be grouped by Issue Type*

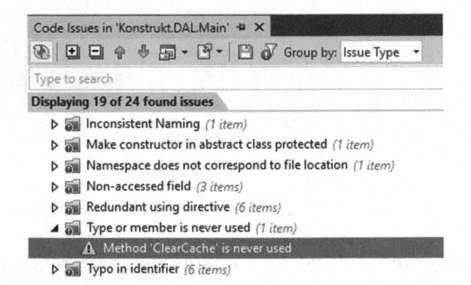

Figure 3-12. *Example results*

If I navigate to the ClearCache method, ReSharper suggests that I remove the ClearCache method which will remove the method from the interface as well. I can also select to comment out the unused method – I'm personally not a big fan of that, and since we have source control, I'll just remove it instead. In total 176 types and members are never used in the example solution – and they might hold on to references to assemblies that are not compatible for our migration. Careful with removing unused classes if you use dependency injection and assembly scanning for autowiring as you might get false positives with the Inspect tool.

Once we've done that, we can proceed with analyzing the reference assemblies in a similar fashion.

Removing Unused References

To avoid false positives when doing the assembly analysis, let's go ahead and remove unused references. This is just as easily done as mentioned earlier – unless you dynamically load assemblies. ReSharper might accidentally remove assemblies that are being used – so tests are going to be important to make sure that we don't remove significant references. If you know that you are loading assemblies dynamically, or you are unsure, be careful with removing assemblies. Make a copy, or better, as suggested earlier, use source control and make commits between changes.

Since we need fine-grained control, we are going to do this one project at a time, centered around the Main project and its dependencies. In the following examples, I'm going to use the BL.Main project.

Select a project and select ReSharper ➤ Find ➤ Optimize References or press Ctrl+Alt+Y (Figure 3-13).

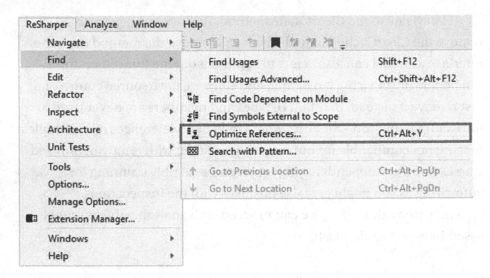

Figure 3-13. *Optimize References can be found in the ReSharper menu*

The result will show different groups depending on the result. For example (Figure 3-14):

- Unused references

- Used references

- Implicit used references

- Unused packages with used dependencies

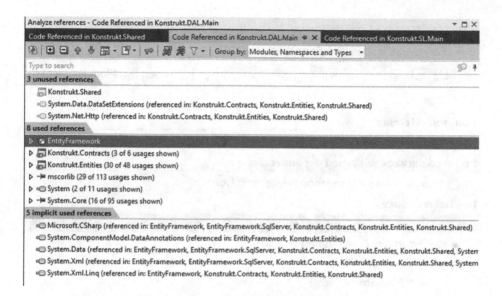

Figure 3-14. *Example results for the data layer project*

We are going to remove the unused references by selecting Remove
unused references icon in the menu in the Analyze References window.
When they are removed, ReSharper will also delete redundant namespace
import directives in the project.

Let's take a look at another project. The Shared project (Figure 3-15).

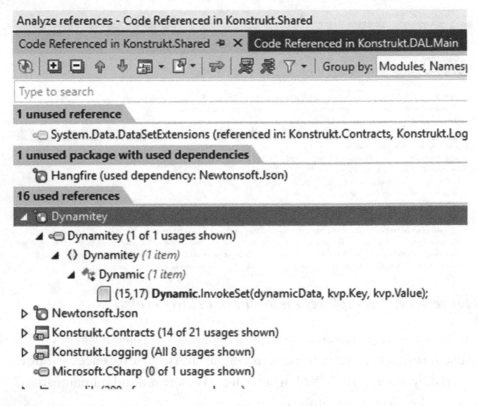

Figure 3-15. *Example results for the Shared project*

In the used references tab, we are going to see if there are any assemblies that aren't used much and can be easily removed.

For this project there is a library Dynamitey (I will get back to this one later) that is used only once – might be worth looking at the usage and decide if we need the library. I'll leave it for now. If you have an assembly that says "showing 0 of X usages," you can take a look at the code dependent on that assembly by using ReSharper. Locate the project in Solution Explorer, and under References find the reference in question and select Find Code Dependent on the Module (Figure 3-16). Example result is shown in Figure 3-17.

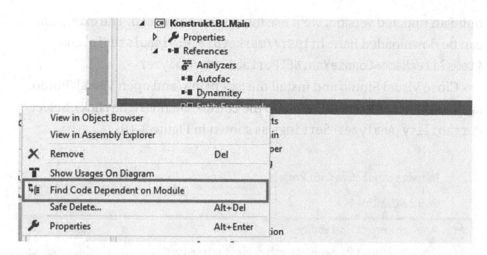

Figure 3-16. *Find Code Dependent on Module can be found in the project context menu if you have ReSharper installed*

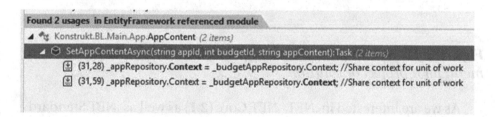

Figure 3-17. *Example results*

The information can help you figure out if the assembly is important, can be replaced, or be removed.

Repeat the preceding steps for all the projects, making sure to clean and build the solution, and run the tests again after each modification. Take notes, and organize them by project and/or namespace. We are going to need the notes for the next part when we run the Portability Analyzer.

We can finally run the `.NET Portability Analyzer` tool. There is an extension for Visual Studio as well as a separate command-line tool that you can use. The latter isn't up to date at the time of writing and has some bugs, and although we could pull down the GitHub repository and build an updated version, we'll use the extension instead. The extension can be downloaded here: `https://marketplace.visualstudio.com/items?itemName=ConnieYau.NETPortabilityAnalyzer`

Close Visual Studio and install the extension, and open Visual Studio again. Select a project and bring up the context menu (right-click). Select `Portability Analyzer Settings` as shown in Figure 3-18.

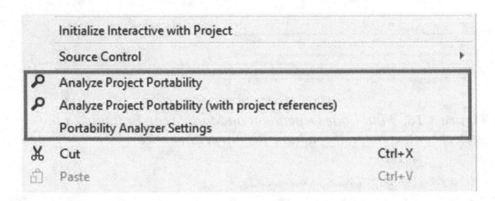

Figure 3-18. Portability Analyzer options can be found in the context menu for a project or solution

As we are interested in .NET, .NET Core (2.1) as well as .NET Standard 2.0, we are going to select those. Close the settings window, and bring up the menu again and this time select `Analyze Project Portability (with project references)` for the SL.Main project. The reason why we are selecting with project references is we want to analyze the portability for the project as a whole – including the dependencies it has – and the service layer is highest up in the tree as we saw in the dependency diagram earlier in this chapter. The analysis should be fairly quick and yield a result Excel sheet as well as quite a few new lines in the `Error List` window. We are going to use both the sheet and the messages in the `Error List` window (Figure 3-19).

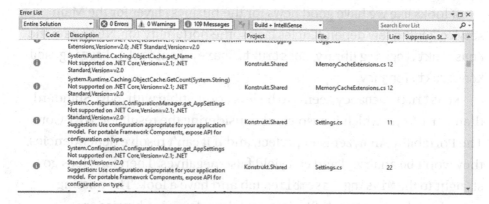

Figure 3-19. *Example results*

Let's start with the Excel sheet. The Excel sheet consists of three tabs:

- Portability Summary

- Details

- Missing Assemblies

Portability Summary

In the first tab, we get a high-level overview (Figure 3-20).

A	B	C	D	E
Submission Id	94162ce2-6aca-4cc4-b769-2cdc1bb0a504			
Description				
Targets	.NET Core,.NET Framework,.NET Standard + Platform Extensions,.NET Standard			
Header for assembly name entries ▼	Target Framework ▼	.NET Core ▼	.NET Framewo ▼	.NET Standard ▼
Konstrukt.BL.Main	.NETFramework,Version=v4.7.2	94.92	100	100
Konstrukt.Contracts	.NETFramework,Version=v4.7.2	100	100	100
Konstrukt.DAL.Main	.NETFramework,Version=v4.7.2	100	100	100
Konstrukt.Entities	.NETFramework,Version=v4.7.2	100	100	100
Konstrukt.Logging	.NETFramework,Version=v4.7.2	86.61	94.64	88.39
Konstrukt.Shared	.NETFramework,Version=v4.7.2	95.55	99.39	98.18
Konstrukt.SL.Main	.NETFramework,Version=v4.7.2	84.35	89.12	87.07
Konstrukt.Tenancy	.NETFramework,Version=v4.7.2	82.45	98.94	100

Figure 3-20. *Summary tab in the analysis Excel file*

It looks like we have good news for the business layer for the Main service. Only a few dependencies lack some portability for .NET Core: the `Konstrukt.Logging` library, `Konstrukt.Share`, `Konstrukt.Logging`, and `Konstrukt.Tenancy`.

`Konstrukt.Tenancy` seems to be less compatible with .NET Standard than .NET Core, which is suspicious considering the result for .NET Core. The Portability Analyzer isn't perfect, and if it can't resolve dependencies, they won't be analyzed and can yield false negatives. Therefore, let's go straight to the `Missing Assemblies` tab and have a look. The missing assemblies for `Konstrukt.BL.Main` and the reference libraries are

- Autofac

- Dynamitey

- EntityFramework

- Log4Net

- Microsoft.ApplicationInsights

- Microsoft.Practices.EnterpriseLibrary. TransientFaultHandling.Data

"Used By" is empty, but we can find which project it is by using Search in Solution Explorer, and afterward "Find Code Dependent on Module" like we did earlier.

The `TransientFaultHandling` is used in the project that maps tenants against the right database, `Konstrukt.Tenancy`. I wrote that library, and I know that it's the `ReliableSQLConnection` type that is used. It shouldn't be a lot of work to write the retry policy ourselves. There is also, as an example, open source libraries that we could use instead such as Polly which supports .NET Standard 1.1. Polly can be downloaded here: `https://github.com/App-vNext/Polly`

Let's go through the rest of them one by one.

Autofac

Autofac is a dependency injection library, and after a quick search I can confirm that it works fine with .NET Core.

Dynamitey

This is an old open source library for working with dynamic objects. It has been quiet on GitHub lately, and we really should remove the dependency on it anyway. Do you remember it from earlier? It was used only once in one project. Let's look at that again, to gage the amount of work to write out the dependency on the Dynamitey library. Here is an example usage:

```
public static void SetFieldName(this IList<dynamic>
data, string fieldName, string fieldValue)
{
    if (data.Count==0) return;
    foreach (var dataItem in data)
    {
        Dynamic.InvokeSet(dataItem, fieldName,
        fieldValue);
    }
}
```

We seem to mainly use the InvokeSet and InvokeGet on the Dynamic type. These two members dynamically invoke the set and get member using the Dynamic Language Runtime (DLR). And we can do that ourselves. We will need some tests as well, so a little bit of work is required.

EntityFramework

EntityFramework(EF), a popular ORM .NET mapper, is a completely different story – we use it heavily and even if we wanted to remove it, we wouldn't be able to do so without a significant rewrite. There is .NET Core version of EF – but EF Core is a complete rewrite of EF, and there are many significant differences between the two. It should not be considered an upgrade. And if you have been using an EDMX model, like we have, then there is even more work. Besides the migration itself, you should expect a lot of time spent testing. The behavior is different, and you might not discover problems until you test all aspects.

To summarize, you have three options in regard to Entity Framework:

- Migrate to EF Core
- Use a different ORM (we have used Dapper in some of our new .NET Core services)
- Migrate to ASP.NET Core but target the full framework

As long as you target the full framework, you can also do a side by side, and run both versions: EF Core and EF6.

Tip   Take a look at the feature comparison chart on MSDN as well as the roadmap on GitHub that is kept up to date. You can find them here: `https://docs.microsoft.com/en-us/ef/efcore-and-ef6/index` and `https://docs.microsoft.com/en-us/ef/core/what-is-new/roadmap`

After discussing it we agreed on an approach where some services will target the full .NET Framework until we can migrate to EF Core and replace EF with a slimmer option such as `Dapper` in services where we don't really use EF for more than object mapping.

Log4Net

At the time of writing, it doesn't implement .NET Standard 2.0, and judging by previous issues, it seems like only file logging would work with earlier versions. NLog on the other hand would be an excellent replacement – and as we have abstracted away the logging, we shouldn't have to do too much work.

Microsoft.ApplicationInsights

Application Insights is a service that Azure provides for application monitoring. It consists of powerful analytics tools and a query language known as Kusto. We use it for performance monitoring, host diagnostics, error monitoring, and more. We want to keep using this Application Performance Management (APM) tool as we haven't found any alternatives that do what we want. Thankfully Microsoft. ApplicationInsights has a .NET Core version found on NuGet: Microsoft. ApplicationInsights.AspNetCore.

Details Tab

Target type	Target member	Header for assembly name entr	.NET Core	.NET Framewo	.NET Standard
T:System.Reflection.Emit.TypeBuilder	T:System.Reflection.Emit.TypeBuilder	Konstrukt.Shared	Supported: 2.0+	Supported: 1.0+	Supported: 1.6+
T:System.Reflection.Emit.TypeBuilder	M:System.Reflection.Emit.TypeBuilder.Creat	Konstrukt.Shared	Supported: 2.0+	Supported: 1.0+	Not supported
T:System.Reflection.Emit.TypeBuilder	M:System.Reflection.Emit.TypeBuilder.Defin	Konstrukt.Shared	Supported: 2.0+	Supported: 1.0+	Supported: 1.6+
T:System.Reflection.Emit.TypeBuilder	M:System.Reflection.Emit.TypeBuilder.Defin	Konstrukt.Shared	Supported: 2.0+	Supported: 1.0+	Supported: 1.6+
T:System.Reflection.Emit.TypeBuilder	M:System.Reflection.Emit.TypeBuilder.Defin	Konstrukt.Shared	Supported: 2.0+	Supported: 1.0+	Supported: 1.6+
T:System.Configuration.ConfigurationManag	T:System.Configuration.ConfigurationManag	Konstrukt.Tenancy	Supported: 3.0+	Supported: 2.0+	Supported: 2.0+
T:System.Configuration.ConfigurationManag	T:System.Configuration.ConfigurationManag	Konstrukt.Logging	Supported: 3.0+	Supported: 2.0+	Supported: 2.0+
T:System.Configuration.ConfigurationManag	T:System.Configuration.ConfigurationManag	Konstrukt.Shared	Supported: 3.0+	Supported: 2.0+	Supported: 2.0+
T:System.Configuration.ConfigurationManag	M:System.Configuration.ConfigurationManag	Konstrukt.Shared	Supported: 3.0+	Supported: 2.0+	Supported: 2.0+
T:System.Configuration.ConfigurationManag	M:System.Configuration.ConfigurationManag	Konstrukt.Shared	Supported: 3.0+	Supported: 2.0+	Supported: 2.0+
T:System.Configuration.ConfigurationManag	M:System.Configuration.ConfigurationManag	Konstrukt.Tenancy	Supported: 3.0+	Supported: 2.0+	Supported: 2.0+
T:System.Configuration.ConfigurationManag	M:System.Configuration.ConfigurationManag	Konstrukt.Logging	Supported: 3.0+	Supported: 2.0+	Supported: 2.0+
T:System.Web.HttpRequest	T:System.Web.HttpRequest	Konstrukt.Shared	Not supported	Supported: 1.0+	Not supported
T:System.Web.HttpRequest	T:System.Web.HttpRequest	Konstrukt.Logging	Not supported	Supported: 1.0+	Not supported
T:System.Web.HttpRequest	M:System.Web.HttpRequest.get_Headers	Konstrukt.Logging	Not supported	Supported: 1.0+	Not supported
T:System.Web.HttpRequest	M:System.Web.HttpRequest.get_Headers	Konstrukt.Shared	Not supported	Supported: 1.0+	Not supported
T:System.Web.HttpRequest	M:System.Web.HttpRequest.get_HttpMetho	Konstrukt.Shared	Not supported	Supported: 1.0+	Not supported
T:System.Reflection.Emit.Label	T:System.Reflection.Emit.Label	Konstrukt.Shared	Supported: 2.0+	Supported: 1.0+	Supported: 1.6+
T:System.Runtime.Caching.ObjectCache	T:System.Runtime.Caching.ObjectCache	Konstrukt.BL.Main	Supported: 3.0+	Supported: 4.0+	Supported: 2.0+
T:System.Runtime.Caching.ObjectCache	T:System.Runtime.Caching.ObjectCache	Konstrukt.Shared	Supported: 3.0+	Supported: 4.0+	Supported: 2.0+
T:System.Runtime.Caching.ObjectCache	T:System.Runtime.Caching.ObjectCache	Konstrukt.Tenancy	Supported: 3.0+	Supported: 4.0+	Supported: 2.0+
T:System.Runtime.Caching.ObjectCache	M:System.Runtime.Caching.ObjectCache.Add	Konstrukt.BL.Main	Supported: 3.0+	Supported: 4.0+	Supported: 2.0+
T:System.Runtime.Caching.ObjectCache	M:System.Runtime.Caching.ObjectCache.Add	Konstrukt.Tenancy	Supported: 3.0+	Supported: 4.0+	Supported: 2.0+
T:System.Runtime.Caching.ObjectCache	M:System.Runtime.Caching.ObjectCache.Cor	Konstrukt.Tenancy	Supported: 3.0+	Supported: 4.0+	Supported: 2.0+
T:System.Runtime.Caching.ObjectCache	M:System.Runtime.Caching.ObjectCache.Get	Konstrukt.BL.Main	Supported: 3.0+	Supported: 4.0+	Supported: 2.0+

Figure 3-21. *The Details tab in the Excel analysis file*

Let's move on to the Details tab as shown in Figure 3-21. This will give us detailed information. For any given assembly, you'll be able to see which type and/or member isn't supported. And in Visual Studio in the Error List window, as an information line under Messages, you can get even more details – and go directly to the file and location in question.

The list is long, but if we take a closer look, it's not as daunting. The main types of issues on the list are

- MemoryCache

- HttpContext

- SQLClient (some unsupported members)

- ExceptionHandlerContext

After some investigation we can conclude the following.

Caching is going to require some rewriting. For .NET Standard there is `Microsoft.Extensions.Caching.Memory`, but the members are quite different and we will have to rewrite our cache management. It requires some work, but doable. `ASP.NET Core MemoryCache` is different from the MemoryCache object in the .NET assembly. There are fewer members available, and you cannot iterate over the cache items. We could explore other options, but at the moment `Microsoft.Extensions.Caching.Memory` seems like a good enough replacement.

The `HttpContext` isn't directly accessible anymore in ASP.NET Core. Instead we will inject the context by using dependency injection. This doesn't require much work at all and is an easy fix that improves our code.

`SQLClient` has some members that are unsupported, but the Microsoft team has been actively working on this issue, and with some temporary workarounds, we should be able to make this work without too much trouble.

For global exception handling in ASP.NET Core, we will need to implement a middleware. Not much work, but it requires some testing.

Summarizing the Work Required for Migrating Konstrukt.BL.Main and Its Dependencies

`Konstrukt.BL.Main` and its dependencies have overall a compatibility with .NET Standard 2.0 as well as .NET Core 2.0. There is some work required such as replacing the logging library, removing the Dynamitey

library and replacing with our own library, possibly migrating to EF
Core or other ORM libraries, rewriting and abstracting our caching logic,
modifying exception handling, and injecting the HTTP context instead of
using it directly. If I had to guestimate, I would say that it would take two
developers 2–3 days to implement the changes and test thoroughly, and an
additional day or two for the data access logic that uses EF.

My colleague Jonas always tells me to then multiply my estimates
by pi. I'm not convinced that's the best way to get an estimate – but he is
right that developers tend to underestimate the amount of work (often
forgetting to take into account the time it takes to debug regression bugs,
random Windows and Visual Studio updates, etc.). The integration and
deployment pipeline also need to be updated – and that can take time.
Obviously, I've already done the work and can tell you how much work it
actually took. As an example, it took me a week to migrate the Main service
(excluding migrating EF). Modifying the pipeline for all the new changes
took 2–3 days.

Analyzing with ICanHasDot.Net

ICanHasDot.Net is a web service by the Octopus Deploy. You provide a
packages file and the service then recursively looks up all the packages
and figures out all the dependencies, direct as well as transitive (indirect).
Then it checks for assembly compatibility against .NET Standard or
PCL (Portable Class Libraries). It gives a clean overview and a pretty
visualization as demonstrated by Figure 3-22. The result summary suggests
replacement libraries and is color coded for easier use.

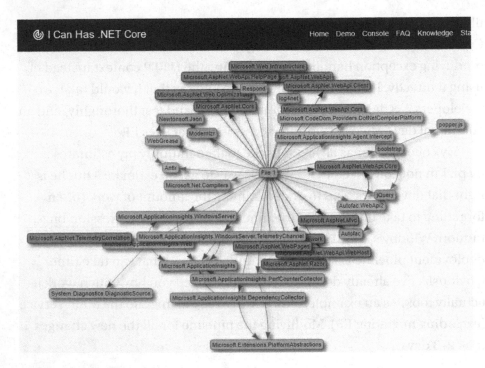

Figure 3-22. *Analysis of Konstrukt.SL.Main*

The GitHub repo has been quiet lately though, so I've started using the tool by the core team instead as my main tool for analyzing the portability of a project. Give the projects a quick go with the tool, but I would recommend that you rely on the tool by the core team as your main source for compatibility information.

Analyzing the Rest of the Solution

For simplicity I'm not going to give you the summarized result from analyzing the rest of the projects as the results are similar to those we got earlier – with a few exceptions.

We have two services that are going to be difficult to migrate. One of them is our Hangfire service which is not included in the example solution. Hangfire is a queue manager for Windows – it lets you set up queues and

queue fire and forget tasks for CPU or I/O intensive tasks that are short-
or long running. Hangfire does not support .NET Standard, but we have
some options nonetheless. One option is to keep the Hangfire service
as is, and not migrate the service. Another option is to replace Hangfire
with something else. The way we use Hangfire is by using it to schedule
API calls to other services that will start tasks such as calculations and
aggregation of data. For our scenario we could replace Hangfire with a
message bus and some infrastructure code – and since we are planning on
adding a message bus to our system, we will probably do that. But for now,
we have decided to leave the service as is and focus on the other services.
Hangfire migration is not something I'm going to cover in this book.

The second challenge, and a bigger one than Hangfire, is our
notification service. Our notification service doesn't do a lot, but the few
things it does are important. The service uses SignalR to initiate WebSocket
connections to update and notify the client of changes and the other way
around. SignalR is not compatible with ASP.NET Core. I've seen attempts
to get it to work with ASP.NET Core with the full framework, but the
SignalR team discourages that. SignalR has been completely rewritten to
ASP.NET Core SignalR (not to be confused with SignalR Core which is a
part of SignalR for the full .NET Framework). SignalR has both a client and
a server, and you would need to replace both, which means we also need
to change our client significantly. This book won't cover the migration of
the SignalR service as that topic deserves its own book.

A Note on the Cost

Before you decide to migrate, it is wise to think about the cost of the
migration – and depending on the size and setup of your team, this might
include the CTO, project manager, and possibly even investors. You should
be leery of something called "resume-driven development."

"Resume-driven development" is when developers and/or architects
select tech stacks, architecture, methodologies, and protocols based on

what looks good on the resume. Often this is not necessarily done with the resume in mind, but we get bored and naturally we like what is new and sexy, and it's tempting to jump on the next new shiny stack, library, or methodology. Information should drive the decision, and unfortunately, I cannot tell you whether or not it is worth it as it depends on several factors. I have however done my best to highlight the factors and provide you with the information and tools to gather the information that you need. One thing remains to discuss before you make that final decision, and that is how to do the migration if you migrate. Partial or full? A partial migration can be less painful and let you test the waters, but at the same time, it adds complexity. In the next chapter, we are going to start planning, and see if the plan holds water.

Summary

In this chapter we did an in-depth analysis and collected data on the work required to do a migration. We have concluded that a migration is doable, but we have yet to decide how before we have a definitive yes or no. We know that we have some services that are going to be harder to migrate and that we will need to redo parts of our data access layer if we want to run ASP.NET Core on .NET Core. At this point we have a fairly good idea of the work required, and in the next chapter we can start planning our migration.

CHAPTER 4

Phase 2: Planning the Architecture

Before we start migrating, it's worth spending some time planning the migration based on what we learned from the analysis we did. Having a plan will save us time, and pain. You certainly don't want to embark on a large migration only to realize halfway through that the approach was wrong and that it's not going to work. Based on my experience, I almost always recommend a gradual migration, but there are cases where a full migration might work. In this chapter we are going to go through the decisions we need to make early on, before migrating.

Available Resources

I work at a startup, and we have a small team that is constantly changing in size (scaling up and down depending on season and outside investment). We have to balance new features to keep our customers and investors happy, with maintenance and managing unintended features (bugs). If we do any sort of rewrite or migration, we have to manage that at the same time as we are doing everything else, and we cannot afford more than a couple of fulltime human resources on a migration or rewrite. Besides the number of available developer hours, you also have to think about knowledge resources. We talked about this earlier, and it's important to

© Iris Classon 2019
I. Classon, *Migrating ASP.NET Microservices to ASP.NET Core*,
https://doi.org/10.1007/978-1-4842-4327-5_4

remember that development will slow down for a while until everybody catches up knowledge wise. You could aim for a few developers that have in-depth knowledge and can help and guide the other developers, or you could get everybody up to date. How and what you and your team choose depend on the size of the team and how work is divided, as well as what the long-term goals are.

What to Migrate

Deciding to migrate is one thing, deciding what to migrate is a different story. You can migrate everything at once, or do a gradual migration which means that you will run ASP.NET Core side by side with ASP.NET services. Decide early on what platforms you want to target, particularly if you want to target cross-platform – or at least have the possibility to do so further down the line. Obviously, if you target cross-platform or a non-Windows platform, you won't be able to use ASP.NET Core targeting the full .NET platform. But you could mix, if you have a distributed system that has different platforms available. Let's talk more about what to migrate.

Migrating Everything

If you have a system that is smaller in size or complexity, or has few dependencies that are not supported, then this option could be for you. Your options are to either target .NET Core directly or target .NET Standard in your libraries and use ASP.NET Core targeting .NET Core for your services. If you want to run ASP.NET Core on the .NET platform instead of .NET Core, you can still use the .NET Standard libraries. I would recommend targeting .NET Standard, as this gives you more flexibility – and you might find out later on that you have to use the libraries in non-. NET Core services or libraries.

For us a full migration was not an option due to the lack of resources and some services that are difficult to migrate.

Gradual Migration and a Mixed System

If you on the other hand, like us, have a large system with intertwined services and/or complex system, then a gradual migration or a mixed-mode system could be a better option. The upside of doing a gradual migration is that it lets you evaluate the expected benefits and distribute resources more evenly. It can also give you an idea how long it takes, although this will vary between services based on size, complexity, and dependencies.

If you are going to maintain a mixed system, you need to decide if you are going to maintain a shared library that targets .NET Standard, or if you want to maintain separate libraries. Sharing libraries is usually preferred if a lot of the code can be shared, and code that differs can be managed with conditional compilation and preprocessor symbols or by using the adapter design pattern.

How to Migrate

Regardless of whether you are migrating the system as a whole or not, you will still need to decide if you are going to migrate the services and the libraries as is or break out logical parts to new services. It makes sense to choose ASP.NET Core, targeting .NET Core or the .NET Framework, for new services unless you have dependencies that won't mix. We have expanded our authentication options this year and added two new services, one for authenticating with SAML2 and one for OpenIdConnect authentication. When we wrote the SAML2 authentication service, we had dependencies that didn't jell well with ASP.NET Core, and therefore we decided to use ASP.NET (hoping to migrate later) for the time being. Our OpenIdConnect service on the other hand is an ASP.NET Core service, targeting .NET Core. It does get confusing, unfortunately, and one way we have tried to solve the confusion is by using different solution files depending on the type of service. I'll get back to this when we talk about the deployment pipeline later in the book.

Migrate Whole Services

We have some services that are fairly well scoped and easy to migrate, such as our Notification service. Besides the bootstrap code and infrastructure code, the classes and libraries could be easily migrated. On the other side, the majority of our services were quite complex and needed more work, and it made sense to try to break out some logical parts to new services.

Break Out Logical Parts to New Services

ASP.NET Core is a good fit for a microservice architecture as it is fast, lightweight, and modular. Ideally your service would be scoped accordingly, but in the real world, services are often parts of a distributed monolith and do a lot of different things. A great example would be our Main service. You can guess just from the name that it does quite a few things. Besides managing user accounts, it also manages user actions such as sharing an App or Plan, logging from the client, and a lot of things I'd rather not share with you as it could potentially give you nightmares. The Main was where the system originated, and somehow everything has ended up there when we didn't know where to put things or were too lazy to create separate services.

The solution for us has been to slowly break out parts to new services, such as our Account services that manage user accounts. Our aim is to have many small, independent services, microservices. I'm not going to go into the details of microservices – that topic deserves a book or ten on its own. In short, I'll mention that many companies have experienced certain problems with monolith systems such as difficulty to scale, long release cycles, difficult to evolve and maintain, as well as long time to add new features. The idea with microservices is that each service does one thing and does that well. Spotify (a music streaming service) is an extreme example, with over 800 active services! Amazon and Walmart are two other excellent examples, and you can find many free articles and videos that they've shared.

Self-Contained Deployment or Framework Dependent

Since we discussed self-contained deployment earlier in the book, I'm going to keep this section short.

When you publish ASP.NET Core services, you can choose between framework-dependent deployment and self-contained deployment. As a quick refresher, self-contained means that your published package will have everything you need to run the service, while the framework-dependent publish will require you to prepare the environment beforehand and install the frameworks. Which one you choose depends on how you manage the environments the service gets deployed to, your user base, as well as whether or not you have size restrictions on your deployment packages.

In short, here are some pros and cons to consider:

Cons

- Need to decide platform and architecture beforehand

- Larger packages

- Publishing can take longer

Pros

- Environment needs less preparation and maintenance

- Ready-to-run packages

- Side-by-side installments

Note   In previous versions of ASP.NET Core and Visual Studio, there were some bugs when creating self-contained packages. If you come across these issues, make sure you have all the Visual Studio updates and are running the latest .NET Core SDK (or runtimes if you don't need the full SDK).

Architecture and Conventions

Lastly, let's not forget the many smaller decisions you need to make in regard to the opinionated framework, ASP.NET Core, such as dependency injection and the logging abstractions. Besides that, there are many other differences that you should keep in mind when planning. Here is an incomplete list of things that differ in ASP.NET Core, some of which caught us by surprise:

- The project file has been simplified and can be opened and edited in Visual Studio without first unloading the project.

- The apps have a different bootstrap mechanism, and Global.asax doesn't exist anymore. The majority of the bootstrapping code is found in the Startup.cs class instead.

- The startup class is loaded through the Main method (similar as in a console app) in the Program.cs file.

- Static files are stored in wwwroot, but can be configured to be stored in a different directory.

- Configuration data can be stored in different file formats, such as JSON files. Instead of the ConfigurationManager.AppSettings, you use the Configuration class that implements IConfiguration to get a section with GetSection. You can also provide a class to map configuration items by using the built-in dependency injection.

- ASP.NET Core has built-in dependency injection, but you can provide your own container resolver (I'll show you how to use Autofac).

- ASP.NET Core has also built-in logging providers, but you can provide your own.

- File access is done through File Providers, and these are used for everything from exposing the content root to locating pages and views (when using Razor Pages).

- App localization is simplified with IStringLocalizer which used the ResourceManager and ResourceReader to manage the culture.

- HttpContext is accessed through IHttpContextAccessor instead of referencing HttpContext.Current directly (I will show you how to inject the context in third-party libraries that are dependent on the HttpContext object).

- ASP.NET Core supports OWIN and utilizes middleware heavily, and it's easy to plug in your own middleware (at a slight performance cost) .

Summary

In this chapter we've taken a look at the migration options that we have and made some decisions in regard to the system we are migrating. We are going to do a partial migration, targeting .NET Core, and opt out of doing a self-contained deployment. There are also smaller decisions that we need to make concerning the architecture and conventions, but we will save that for the next chapter and cover them as we do the migration.

CHAPTER 5

Phase 3: Migration

I've taken part in many different types of migrations and rewrites – it seems like most developers will encounter a similar situation sooner or later. User expectations are quickly changing as technology is evolving, and as programming is becoming more popular, the pool of libraries and platforms to choose between is growing. Not only is it tempting to migrate so we can try new solutions, it is often necessary to keep up with expectations and the growing technology stack. I've seen some migrations go really bad, and what they often had in common was lack of planning and unclear end goals. Fortunately for us we have done an extensive analysis and planned the migration. This helps us create a roadmap that we can refer to so we know where we are and where we are going.

These are the migration steps I recommend, based on your end goal.

Full Migration

Create the ASP.NET Core projects as well as libraries you might have (not third party). If you are targeting the full .NET Framework or if you want to consume the libraries by .NET Framework libraries, then I would target .NET Standard. .NET Standard gives you more freedom, but also more work.

Create the unit and integration test projects. As mentioned earlier, if you plan on consuming parts of the system by .NET Framework libraries (as well as .NET Core), then you will have to test against all the platforms that you support. Methods and types not supported on a particular

I. Classon, *Migrating ASP.NET Microservices to ASP.NET Core*,
https://doi.org/10.1007/978-1-4842-4327-5_5

platform will throw a PlatformNotSupportedException which will help you discover issues early on. I'll cover in detail how this can be done later in this chapter.

Given a simple setup with one web service, a library, and a unit test library, you would aim for the following end result (Figure 5-1).

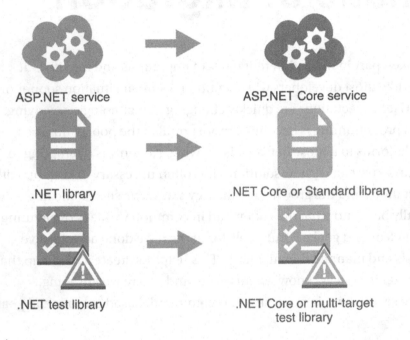

Figure 5-1. *What to aim for in a full migration with a simple setup*

If you have several ASP.NET services, I would start with just one of them, migrate own dependencies, and then resolve third-party dependencies. There is no particular order I would recommend, but if your application is database driven, a good place to start would be with the data access layer. Otherwise start with the libraries with the least amount of third-party dependencies.

Afterward I would proceed with migrating the test projects that test the logic in the libraries you migrated, followed by migrating the ASP.NET service and tests that test the logic in the ASP.NET service.

Note   Use a dependency graph (see Figure 5-3 for an example) to visualize the dependencies so you know what the dependencies are. ReSharper, for example, adds an option in the Solution Explorer context menu to display a project dependency graph.

Rinse and repeat for other services and dependencies that they have.

Partial Migration

The main difference between doing a full and partial migration is that you need to make sure that dependencies you migrate that are used by other libraries or services that are not migrated can still be used and work as expected. You might also choose to break out parts of a service or a library and only migrate that part, and you will have to run tests for all the targeted platforms. With a partial migration, you also have to maintain a mixed continuous integration and deployment pipeline. The migration I'm going to walk you through (Figure 5-2) is a partial migration as it is more challenging. Everything we are doing also applies to a full migration, minus extra considerations.

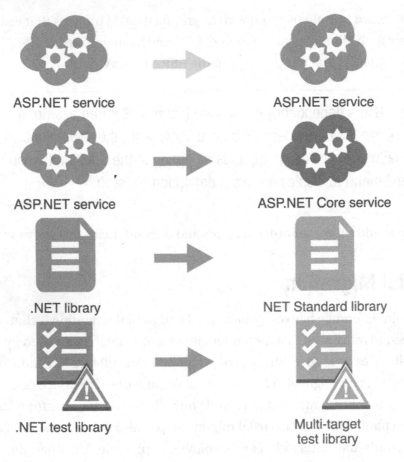

Figure 5-2. *Example of a partial migration*

Partial Migration Walkthrough

Let's recap what we are going to migrate and what we want to achieve. At the moment the solution has three services, five libraries (our own), some unit test libraries, and a helper library for test libraries as shown to the left in Figure 5-3. The end goal can be seen on the right (Figure 5-3).

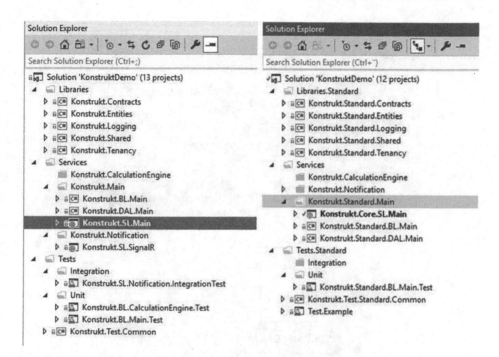

Figure 5-3. *Starting point for the example solution is shown on the left, compared to the migrated result shown on the right*

In this walkthrough we are going to migrate the Main service, which has dependencies on libraries that are used by other services that we won't be migrating.

I always recommend looking at a dependency graph to better understand how things are connected. Sometimes it's not obvious what dependencies a service has, as a graph can be quite deep. A dependency graph also helps us locate a good place to start – often at the outer edges of the graph. Figure 5-4 shows us the dependency graph for the Konstrukt. SL.Main service. You can get a dependency graph by right-clicking a project in Solution Explorer in Visual Studio, if you have the ReSharper plugin installed.

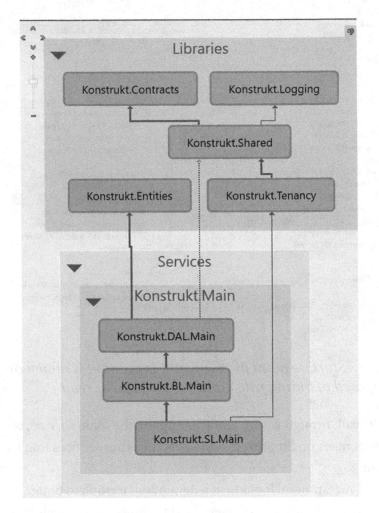

Figure 5-4. *Konstrukt.SL.Main dependency graph*

Based on the dependency graph, we are going to do this migration by starting with one of the outer dependencies with the least third-party dependencies and then work our way toward the ASP.NET service itself including the unit tests.

High-level overview:

Every library is migrated to a new .NET Standard (except the service itself) library. The references to the old library are then updated to the new library, and after verifying that everything compiles and the tests are green, the old library is deleted. For each section we do a Git commit so we can easily revert a change if something went wrong. We only push to origin once we can verify that the solution compiles and the tests are green.

Steps:

Migrate Konstrukt.Contracts

Migrate Konstrukt.Share

Migrate Konstrukt.Logging

Migrate Test.Common

Run old tests with new Test.Common library

Delete old Test.Common library

Attempt to migrate Test library

Migrate Konstrukt.Tenancy

Migrate Konstrukt.Entities (including migrating Entity Framework to Entity Framework Core)

Migrate Konstrukt.DAL.Main

Migrate Konstrukt.BL.Main

Migrate Test library

Migrate Konstrukt.SL.Main

Migrating Contracts

The Contracts library is the first one to be migrated. We need to make an important decision before we begin, and that is how to organize the code. We can keep the projects in a separate solution, or in the same solution. For this example, we will keep them in the same solution as we migrate, but we are going to discuss the pros and cons of using several solution files later in this book. The second thing we need to decide on is naming conventions. Somehow, we need to separate the new libraries from the old ones, and as we will have two similar libraries side by side until we can verify everything was migrated correctly, we won't be able to use the same names anyway. As you know, on Windows, a path can get too long, so if the project resides in a nested folder, you can get problems down the line. With .NET Core and .NET Standard projects, you might get mysterious errors in regard to restoring packages such as "Operation failed as details for project could not be loaded," when the problem is the path.

For this migration, as an example, we will be creating a solution folder for .NET Standard libraries and prefix the libraries with "Standard". You can see in the earlier side-by-side comparison of the solution before and after how the libraries and services are organized. Let's get started!

Create a new project targeting .NET Standard under a folder called Libraries.Standard as shown in Figure 5-5. All the projects will be .NET Standard projects as we have other .NET libraries and services dependent on them. The exception is the ASP.NET Core service that will target .NET Core and the Unit Test library that will target both the .NET platform and .NET Core.

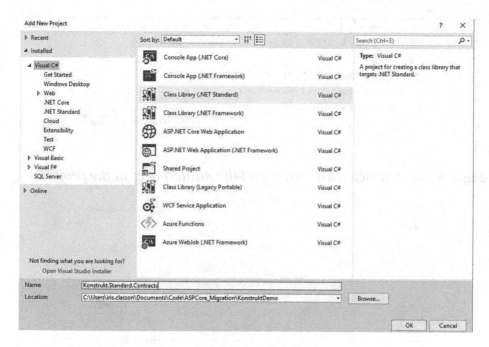

Figure 5-5. *Creating a new .NET Standard library*

Delete the Class1.cs file and copy over the files from the old Contracts project. You can copy over just a folder, or a few files, or all. It's really up to you, and you might want to weigh the size of the project and how dependent on each other the files are. Contracts is a small library, so we will copy over all the files and folders.

Open up a random file, set the marker on the namespace that should have a blue squiggly line underlining the namespace, and bring up the ReSharper helper (Alt+Enter). Select Move to, and use arrow to select Adjust namespaces in project (Figure 5-6). If it suggests opening all the files so it can be undone, select No (Figure 5-7).

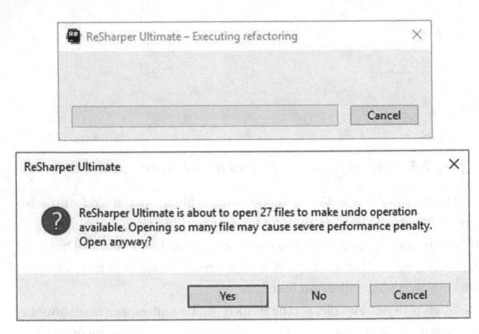

Figure 5-6. *Shortcut to adjusting all the namespaces in the project*

Figure 5-7. *Opening all the edited files might leave Visual Studio unresponsive*

If there are many files, Visual Studio might crash. Do instead a Git commit before and after, as you can always revert the latest commit if something goes wrong.

Next step is to fix everything that generates an error, such as missing references, and in this example it's fairly straightforward. Open the Error List window, and filter for "Current Project," and use the list as a guide (Figure 5-8).

Figure 5-8. *The Error List window has filtering options such as filter for current project*

The keyboard shortcut F8 will take you to the next error in the list, and Shift+F8 will go to the previous.

If you land on a red reference, Alt+Enter at that location should bring up the ReSharper helper. Among the suggestions, you'll see "Find this type on nuget.org" (Figure 5-9). This works, sometimes, and if you want to give it a try, select that option and scroll through the list.

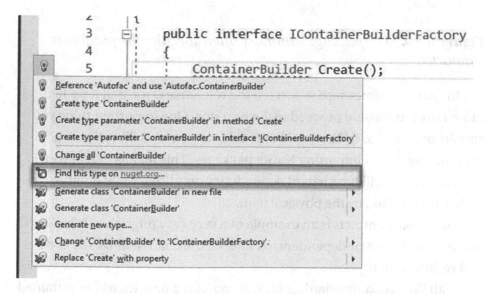

Figure 5-9. *ReSharper provides a shortcut menu for NuGet searches*

Once you find the package in the list, expand information by clicking the + icon, and make sure that .NET Standard is supported (Figure 5-10). If it does, click the download icon and download the package. Another option is to do a manual search using the package manager.

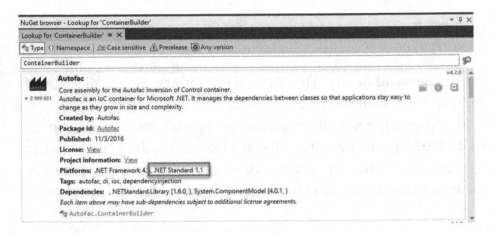

Figure 5-10. *The package summary often specifies the platforms supported*

Import the namespace to sort out the reference error, and if we had more errors, we would proceed to the next one. One important thing you should know is that ReSharper likes to add references to libraries in a solution, instead of importing NuGet packages. This means that in your project file, you will have a hard dependency on a library that another library uses, linked by the physical path.

Konstrukt.Contracts is an example of a very easy migration. It had no unsupported types or dependencies, and we only had to move the code and rename namespaces.

With Konstrukt.Standard.Contracts compiling fine, we will now unload the Konstrukt.Contracts project (instead of deleting it) by right-clicking that project and selecting "Unload project." This should result in many errors, from the projects that have a dependency on it. We will view the Error List as our to-do list.

Konstrukt.Share is one of the projects that has a dependency on Konstrukt.Contracts. We can see that the imported namespaces are red as the dependency can't be resolved.

For the project, select References and remove Konstrukt.Contracts and add Konstrukt.Standard.Contracts instead. The errors are still there as the previous namespace doesn't correspond to the new one. We can sort this out in two ways. One is by using "Search and Replace," the second is by using ReSharper.

Search and Replace

Bring up Search and Replace (Ctrl+F, then expand the window), set it to "Current Project," and do a search and replace for Konstrukt.Contracts to Konstrukt.Standard.Contracts (Figure 5-11).

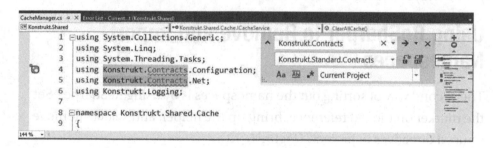

Figure 5-11. *Search and Replace can help speed up the migration to new namespaces*

Enabling undo can cause Visual Studio to crash, and if we do a Git commit instead, we can skip enabling undo and risk Visual Studio not responding for a while (Figure 5-12).

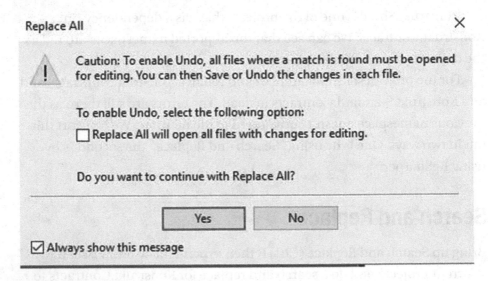

Figure 5-12. *Opening all the edited files can cause performance problems for Visual Studio*

Using ReSharper to Remove and Import Namespaces

The second way of sorting out the namespaces is by using ReSharper. Set the marker on the red reference, bring up the helper, and select "Remove unused directives in project" (Figure 5-13).

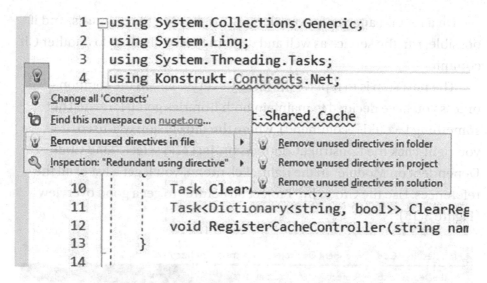

```
1  ☐using System.Collections.Generic;
2   using System.Linq;
3   using System.Threading.Tasks;
4   using Konstrukt.Contracts.Net;
```

☐ Change all 'Contracts'
☐ Find this namespace on nuget.org...   t.Shared.Cache
☐ Remove unused directives in file   ▶   ☐ Remove unused directives in folder
☐ Inspection: "Redundant using directive"   ▶   ☐ Remove unused directives in project
                                                  ☐ Remove unused directives in solution

```
10  :  :       Task Clear
11  :  :       Task<Dictionary<string, bool>> ClearReg
12  :  :       void RegisterCacheController(string nam
13  :  }
14  :
```

Figure 5-13. *ReSharper has a shortcut menu for removing unused namespaces*

If you go to a missing type that is marked red, you can import missing references in project (Figure 5-14). I would caution you to only use this after making sure that you have a reference to that project or a NuGet package for that namespace.

```
11  :  }
12  :
13  ☐:  public class CacheService : ICacheService
14  :  {
                            ● Import 'Konstrukt.Standard.Contracts.Net.IApiHttpClient' and other
15  :      readonly IApiHttpClient _apiHttpClient;
```

☐ Import missing references in file   ▶   ☐ Import missing references in folder
☐ Import type 'Konstrukt.Standard.Contracts.Net.IApiHttpClient' ▶   ☐ Import missing references in project   l(
☐ Create interface 'IApiHttpClient'   ☐ Import missing references in solution
☐ Create nested interface 'IApiHttpClient'
☐ Create type parameter 'IApiHttpClient' in class 'CacheService'   iHttpClient apiHttpClient, :
☐ Change all 'IApiHttpClient'
                                                                    iHttpClient;

Figure 5-14. *There is also a shortcut for importing missing namespaces*

Do a rebuild and verify everything is alright. Run the unit tests, and if possible, run the service as well and do some test calls, and do another Git commit.

The next step is to replace the library everywhere in the solution – unless you have decided to maintain both libraries going forward (not something I would recommend), where the old version was used. If you right-click the Konstrukt.Contracts project and select "Find Code Dependent on Module" in the right-click menu, you'll get a list of all the references. Use the Group by "Project Structure" to get a good overview (Figure 5-15).

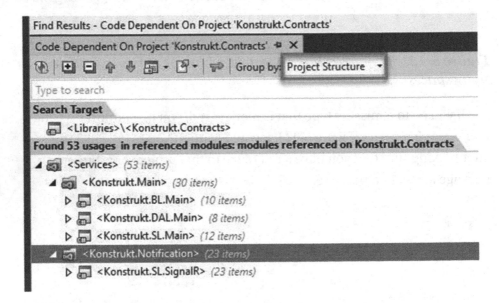

Figure 5-15. *Grouping by project structure*

We have four more projects to make changes to:

- Konstrukt.BL.Main

- Konstrukt.DAL.Main

- Konstrukt.SL.Main

- Konstrukt.SL.SignalR

We will have to repeat the preceding steps, going one project at a time, and doing a Git commit between each. Build, verify no errors, run the tests, and run the services. Obviously, this means a lot of clicking around, and therefore I would recommend that you assign a keyboard shortcut for Add Reference.

In the main menu, go to Tools ➤ Options ➤ Environment ➤ Keyboard as shown in Figure 5-16.

Set command type to AddReference and select a combination. I used Ctrl+Shift+Alt+R. Assign, and you are good to go.

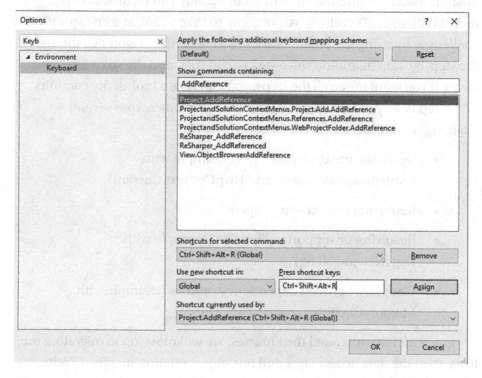

Figure 5-16. *You can create your own shortcuts in the Keyboard section*

You could also manually edit the project files, if you prefer that. But do not forget to build and test between changes, and do frequent commits.

Verify that Konstrukt.Contracts is not referenced anywhere, and delete it. Open up File Explorer and make sure the project truly is deleted. Deleting from Visual Studio usually only removed it from the solution file, but the folder and the project are still there and will be checked in next time you do a Git push. Save all, build and run tests, and if everything is fine, do a commit.

The Contracts library was easy to migrate as it didn't have any unsupported dependencies or types, but usually you'll come across more challenges. Therefore, we are going to take a look at some specific challenges by using the other libraries as an example. I won't go through the step-by-step migration since we just did that, and the steps are the same. If you want to see all the steps, you can take a look at my commits in the repository. While migrating the rest, we came across several challenges; here are some that I'll cover:

- Resolving unsupported types (example with ConfigurationManager and HttpContext.Current)

- Removing unnecessary dependencies

- Resolving unsupported libraries (example with Log4Net and NLog)

- Choosing between dependency options (example with MemoryCache)

Once we have migrated the libraries, we will move on to migrating the tests, then the data access layer and our object relation mapper (Entity Framework), before we finally migrate the ASP.NET service itself.

Missing Type: ConfigurationManager

The heading is a little bit misleading, as the type is not missing anymore. But it was missing until .NET Standard 2.0. I wanted to include this example as we have several options in regard to how we deal with accessing configuration settings. In earlier versions of .NET Core and Standard, this type was not available. The team encouraged the use of dependency injection to access configuration settings.

This is done by creating a class that maps to the settings you want to access, and the settings are then accessed by using IOptions<MyCustomSettings>. If you decide on using JSON files for settings in your services, the dependency injection is a better option (generally I would recommend that over specific types that pull in dependencies). Otherwise you could also use the IConfiguration interface and the GetSection method if you don't want to use a mapping class. In Konstrukt.Standard.Shared we have a Settings class that is used to access settings in configuration files. This class could be rewritten for .NET Core using the two preceding options. However, as we want to support several platforms, we need a generic solution. Prior to .NET Standard 2.0, two ways of dealing with this would have been to either use conditional compilation or dependency injection. But the luck is on our side, and there is now a NuGet package that we can use, so we are going to use that for now.

We can always go back at a later point and refactor away that dependency and transient dependencies. As you can see, there are a few.

Remember that you have to choose your battles, and sometimes a less than ideal option is the best as there are other issues pressing that will take a lot of time. At the same time, you don't want to have to maintain unnecessary dependencies.

Rewriting to Avoid Unnecessary Dependencies

The Shared library has an extension method, ToDynamicObject, that uses a library that until recently didn't support .NET Standard – Dynamitey. The support was added a year ago, but it hadn't been maintained for several years prior to that. I'd rather not have a dependency on a library if we only use a very small part of it, and it's something we can do ourselves. There is an interesting story about a Node.js package called Pad-Left. It was only a few lines of JavaScript, and all it did was – you guess it – pad left. It was used everywhere, and when the author removed the package from the NPM, the Internet was broken for a day. Pulling in a library for something very simple is now something I refer to as doing a "pad-left." The less dependencies you have, the easier the migration, and also, you might avoid sudden breaking changes when doing an update.

In our case the InvokeSet is only used for creating a dynamic object from a dictionary and can be rewritten from

```
public static dynamic ToDynamicObject(this
Dictionary<string, object> data)
{
    dynamic dynamicData = new ExpandoObject();
    foreach (var kvp in data)
    {
        Dynamic.InvokeSet(dynamicData, kvp.Key,
        kvp.Value);
    }
    return dynamicData;
}
```

to

```
public static dynamic ToDynamicObject2(this
Dictionary<string, object> data)
{
    IDictionary<string, object> dynamicData = new
    ExpandoObject();
    foreach (var kvp in data)
    {
        dynamicData.Add(kvp);
    }
    return dynamicData;
}
```

Don't be afraid to rewrite, but do make sure that you have plenty of tests! And as I mentioned before – pick your battles wisely.

Missing Type: HttpContext.Current

We got in a bad habit of passing around the HTTP context in our libraries. It created hard dependencies, could cause additional issues if we worked with several threads and lost the original thread context, and many other issues.

Accessing the HttpContext from other libraries is not an ideal thing to do; the HTTP context should really be scoped to the service itself, and passing it around in external libraries creates a messy architecture. This is why you won't find this type in ASP.NET Core. The HTTP context is instead accessed through the HttpContextAccessor type, by using dependency injection and the interface IHttpContextAccessor. You can find some ugly workarounds so you can keep using HttpContext.Current (sort of), but let me show you how easy it is to solve our problem with dependency injection. This is the class we need to refactor:

```
public class CurrentRequest : ICurrentRequest
{
    readonly Regex _subDomainRegex = new Regex(@"^(htt
    ps?:\/\/)?([^\.]+)", RegexOptions.Compiled);

    public string Origin =>
        HttpContext.Current.Request.Headers["X-Origin"] ??
        HttpContext.Current.Request.Headers["Origin"] ??
        HttpContext.Current.Request.Headers["Referer"];

    public string Authorization =>
        HttpContext.Current.Request.Headers["Authorization"];

    public string HttpMethod =>
        HttpContext.Current.Request.HttpMethod;

    public string SubDomain =>
        _subDomainRegex.Match(Origin).Groups[2].Value;
}
```

We can create an interface called IRequest:

```
public interface IRequest
{
    NameValueCollection Headers();
    string HttpMethod { get; }
}
```

Which will then be injected in the CurrentRequest constructor:

```
public class CurrentRequest : ICurrentRequest
{
    private readonly IRequest _request;
```

```
public CurrentRequest(IRequest request)
{
    _request = request;
}
readonly Regex _subDomainRegex = new Regex(@"^
(https?:\/\/)?([^\.]+)", RegexOptions.Compiled);

public string Origin =>
    _request.Headers()["X-Origin"] ??
    _request.Headers()["Origin"] ??
    _request.Headers()["Referer"];

public string Authorization =>
    _request.Headers()["Authorization"];

public string HttpMethod
    => _request.HttpMethod;

public string SubDomain =>
    _subDomainRegex.Match(Origin).Groups[2].Value;
}
```

When we use this, we only have to have a custom type that implements that interface, and for a standard ASP.NET application, we can do the following:

```
public class SlimRequest : IRequest
{
    public NameValueCollection Headers() => HttpContext.
Current.Request.Headers;
    public string HttpMethod => HttpContext.Current.Request.
HttpMethod;
}
```

For an ASP.NET Core application:

```
public class SlimRequest : IRequest
{
    private readonly IHttpContextAccessor _httpContextAccessor;

    public SlimRequest(IHttpContextAccessor
    httpContextAccessor)=>
        _httpContextAccessor = httpContextAccessor;

    public NameValueCollection Headers()
    {
        var collection = new NameValueCollection();

        foreach (var item in _httpContextAccessor.HttpContext.
        Request.Headers)
            collection.Add(item.Key, item.Value);

        return collection;
    }

    public string HttpMethod => _httpContextAccessor.
HttpContext.Request.Method;
}
```

Dependency Options: New vs. Old MemoryCache

MemoryCache was one of those types that weren't supported until later in
.NET Core and .NET Standard. The library System.Runtime.Caching has
a MemoryCache object that we are used to using in ASP.NET. In ASP.NET
Core caching is better integrated and is done by using an IMemoryCache
service. Different caches are supported with the most basic one being the
IMemoryCache which supports any object value. The object returned by
the service resides in the Microsoft.Extensions.Caching.Memory assembly.

The MemoryCache object there differs significantly from the one we are used to from the System.Runtime.Caching assembly.

While the Microsoft.Extensions.Caching.Memory.MemoryCache is recommended over the other one as it is better integrated with ASP. NET Core, System.Runtime.Caching.MemoryCache might be better for compatibility reasons when you are migrating. Both of them are compatible with .NET Standard 2.0 – which means that you can use either in a .NET Standard 2.0 (and up) library such as the ones we are migrating to. You can read more about the two options here: https://github.com/aspnet/Docs/blob/master/aspnetcore/performance/caching/memory.md

In the Shared library, we have a class called MemoryCacheExtensions. It has one method that iterates through a MemoryCache object and outputs the keys.

```
public static CacheStatistics Statistics(this MemoryCache
cache)
{
    return new CacheStatistics
    {
        Name = cache.Name,
        NumberOfObjects = cache.GetCount(),
        Items = cache.Select(s =>
        {
            var info = s.Key;
            var list = s.Value as IEnumerable;
            if (list != null)
                info += ", Count: " + Count(list);
            return info;
        })
    };
}
```

The Microsoft.Extensions.Caching.Memory.MemoryCache doesn't let you iterate through the keys (something that some developers disagree with, but the team has decided to not allow this nonetheless) as the keys might have changed. It makes sense from a usage perspective, but we have been using the Statistics extension for diagnostic reasons as we often have problems with our cache(s). There are hacks you could use to work around this limitation if you want to iterate through the keys, but since we also make use of other members not supported (such as .Contains()) in our cache handlers, we will use the System.Runtime.Caching.MemoryCache which is recommended when porting or migrating from legacy to core.

Replacing Dependencies: Logging

To finish migrating the Shared library, we need to have a logger. The logging has been managed by a separate library, called Konstrukt.Logging. The logging adapter we used was Log4Net, a popular open source library that has been around for ages. The library is however a little bit slow to adapt and adopt changes and, at the time of writing, has yet to support database logging if you use .NET Core. Therefore, we are going to replace Log4Net with NLog, a very similar library that is quite performant and supports .NET Standard 1.6 and up.

The only thing I had to do was create a new project, Konstrukt.Share. Logging, add a reference to NLog, and set up the code and configuration. I also made sure that the log messages follow the same pattern in the database as Log4Net, so we can use the existing database. I added a temporary class that wraps the global exception handler as a workaround until we've migrated the service.

Although the configuration is in the logging library, I made sure to set the database at startup in Global.asax.cs and renamed the connection string from Log4Net to NLog and removed Log4Net references. We are going to change this later for our ASP.NET Core service.

```
LogManager.Configuration.Variables["configurationDb"]
= ConfigurationManager.ConnectionStrings["NLog"].
ConnectionString;
```

The ApplicationInsights reference is updated for one that supports .NET Standard (Microsoft.ApplicationInsights), and no rewrite is needed.

Static Logging Instance vs. Dependency Injection

For various reasons we chose to go with a static logger instance, although using dependency injection is also a popular way of accessing a logging object. As a matter of fact, that is the recommended way in ASP.NET Core. However, so we won't have to rewrite large parts of our code and start injecting our logger instead of using a static instance, we are going to migrate the logging as is for now. Later in the migrating process, I'm going to show you how to use dependency injection with the logger. As I've mentioned before, our logging is not done to a file, but to a database, and therefore we don't have to worry as much about concurrency.

Migrating Unit Tests

.NET Standard is, as we discussed earlier, a specification and not a platform. Therefore, if we want to write tests, we need to target the platforms that we want our test projects to support. If we only targeted .NET Core, then we could have created .NET Core test libraries, but since we have shared libraries, we want to make sure we are testing for the right platforms.

Our first step is migrating any helper libraries the test libraries might have. We have, for example, Test.Common. This library sets up our dependency mocker. Migrating this library to .NET Standard is easy, as all the third-party libraries it depends on are supported. After replacing references to the old Test.Common library, we can verify that all the tests run without problems, with the expected results. If you have unit test projects that only test code in libraries that are already ported, and have no dependencies on platform-specific libraries, then you can migrate those tests. You create a .NET Standard library (we will be changing this later) and plug in the references that you need, including the Test.Common library.

If you at any point get the error shown in Figure 5-17, you need to run a package restore.

	Code	Description	Project ▲	▼	File	Line	Suppress
❌	CS0246	The type or namespace name 'System' could not be found (are you missing a using directive or an assembly reference?)	Konstrukt.BL.Main.Test.St...		.NETStandard,Version=v2...	2	Active
❌	CS0246	The type or namespace name 'System' could not be found (are you missing a using directive or an assembly reference?)	Konstrukt.BL.Main.Test.St...		.NETStandard,Version=v2...	3	Active
❌	CS0400	The type or namespace name 'System' could not be found in the global namespace (are you missing an assembly reference?)	Konstrukt.BL.Main.Test.St...		.NETStandard,Version=v2...	4	Active
❌	CS0518	Predefined type 'System.String' is not defined or imported	Konstrukt.BL.Main.Test.St...		.NETStandard,Version=v2...	4	Active
❌	CS0246	The type or namespace name 'FrameworkDisplayName' could not be found (are you missing a using directive or an assembly reference?)	Konstrukt.BL.Main.Test.St...		.NETStandard,Version=v2...	4	Active
❌	CS0518	Predefined type 'System.String' is not defined or imported	Konstrukt.BL.Main.Test.St...		.NETStandard,Version=v2...	4	Active
❌	CS0246	The type or namespace name 'System' could not be found (are you missing a using directive or an assembly reference?)	Konstrukt.BL.Main.Test.St...		Class1.cs	1	Active
❌	CS0518	Predefined type 'System.Object' is not defined or imported	Konstrukt.BL.Main.Test.St...		Class1.cs	5	Active
❌	CS0246	The type or namespace name 'System' could not be found (are you missing a using directive or an assembly reference?)	Konstrukt.BL.Main.Test.St...		Konstrukt.BL.Main.Test.St...	11	Active
❌	CS0246	The type or namespace name 'System' could not be found (are you missing a using directive or an assembly reference?)	Konstrukt.BL.Main.Test.St...		Konstrukt.BL.Main.Test.St...	12	Active

Figure 5-17. *CS0246: The type or namespace name System could not be found*

Open the NuGet Package Manager Console and run "dotnet restore."

Here is a very simple example with a project called Test.Example. The project tests the LoggedInUserRetriever in Shared. The project has the following dependencies:

- NUnit

- Moq

- Konstrukt.Test.Standard.Common

- Konstrukt.Standard.Shared

The "ArrangeBase" base class sets up the mocks, other configurations, as well as the subject tested (LoggedInUserRetriever):

```
namespace Test.Example.Given_LoggedInUserRetriever
{
    public class Arrange : ArrangeBase<LoggedInUserRetriever>
    {
        protected virtual string UserName => "SomeUser";

        [SetUp]
        public void Init()
        {
            DependencyMocker.MockOf<IPrincipal>().SetupGet
            (x => x.Identity.Name).Returns(UserName);
        }
    }
}
```

This base class setup is shared across the unit tests in the Given_ LoggedInUserRetriever folder, but the virtual members can be overridden in the classes that inherit from this class.

The ArrangeBase.cs resides in Test.Standard.Common and is a base class that automagically mocks injected dependencies for the given type through the type DependencyMocker. The type defined is set as the Subject of the unit tests. In the Init() method, we set up specific mocks, and in this example we want the IPrincipal that is injected in the class we are testing to have the username "SomeUser". When_User_Is_Logged_ In.cs has just one test that asserts that the result from acting on the GetLoggedInUserId() method on the Subject (LoggedInUserRetriever) returns the expected username, in this case "SomeUser".

The example is simple, it's just to have a test to run – and to show more complex unit test setup as most systems have complex setups for their tests and mocks. At this point we can't actually run the tests. We created the project as a .NET Standard library, and therefore NUnit can't know which platform to run the test on. We need to change that. This is done in the project file. The new csproj file is easier to work with than it used to be with .NET projects. Instead of having to unload the project to edit the file, we can simply edit it directly. You'll see a section called TargetFramework, and the section is set to netstandard2.0. Since we want to support two platforms, .NET Core 2.0 and .NET4.7.1, we add those instead, separated by a semicolon, and change the element to plural – TargetFrameworks.

```
<TargetFrameworks>netcoreapp2.0;net472</TargetFrameworks>
```

You also need to add two other NuGet packages, the NUnit3TestAdapter and the Microsoft.NET.Test.SDK. Do this through the package manager or by using a PackageReference in the project file:

```
<ItemGroup>
  <PackageReference Include="nunit" Version="3.10.1" />
  <PackageReference Include="NUnit3TestAdapter"
Version="3.10.0" />
  <PackageReference Include="Microsoft.NET.Test.Sdk"
Version="15.7.2" />
</ItemGroup>
```

You should now be able to run the tests, and they will be run for both target platforms (Figure 5-18).

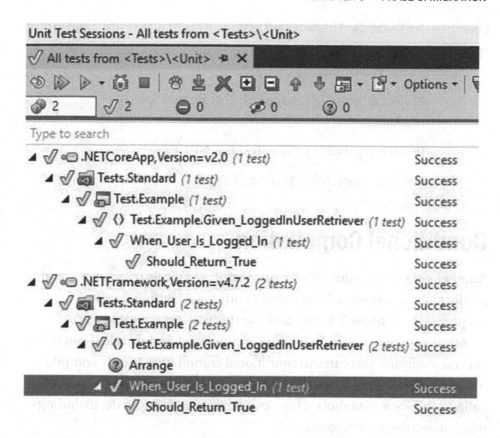

Figure 5-18. *Running unit tests for a project that targets several platforms*

For some odd reason, the Test Explorer thinks that the Arrange class has a test; it doesn't so just ignore it if you get an extra test when you use a base class. As long as the number for All Tests and Passed Tests matches, you should be good. Unfortunately, there are still a few bugs with the Test Explorer and the ReSharper extension.

Projects that target a specific platform should have tests that test against that specific platform. This means that you'll most likely end up with several test projects, some that target several platforms as they test code in a .NET Standard library, and test projects that only test code for specific platforms.

Here is what you could do:

Project targets .NET Standard: Test for multiple platforms

Project targets .NET Core: Test for .NET Core

Project targets .NET: Test for .NET

Conditional Compilation

Another alternative, popular with open source projects targeting several platforms, is to use something called conditional compilation and preprocessor symbols. You can also use this when you have to use a different implementation depending on the target framework. If you target several platforms, you can use conditional compilation to only compile a section of code for a specific platform. This is done by using something called compilation symbols. These can be used with any code, including when importing namespaces.

```
#if NET472
using Konstrukt.BL.Main;
#else
using Konstrukt.Standard.BL.Main;
#endif
```

You could even have more complicated logic. Here is a typical example from the popular Newtonsoft library:

```
#if !(NET20 || NET35 || PORTABLE40 || PORTABLE) ||
NETSTANDARD1_3 || NETSTANDARD2_0
using System.Numerics;
#endif
```

The target frameworks and symbols can be found here:

https://docs.microsoft.com/en-us/dotnet/csharp/language-reference/preprocessor-directives/preprocessor-if

You could use conditional compilation directly in your tests, and even wrap whole tests so they are only run for certain platforms. This does however mean that code coverage will differ, and it's not very obvious by just looking at the tests – not to mention that this can get really messy. If you decide to go this route, make sure that you have thought this thoroughly and considered other options. Don't use this as a quick fix, as it will come back and bite you.

Adding conditional project references is done in the csproj file like this:

```
<ItemGroup Condition=" '$(TargetFramework)' == 'net472' ">
    <Reference Include="System.Net" />
    <ProjectReference Include="Konstrukt.BL.Main" />
</ItemGroup>
```

When you are working in a file, you can select the platform you want IntelliSense for from the left drop-down for the file (Figure 5-19).

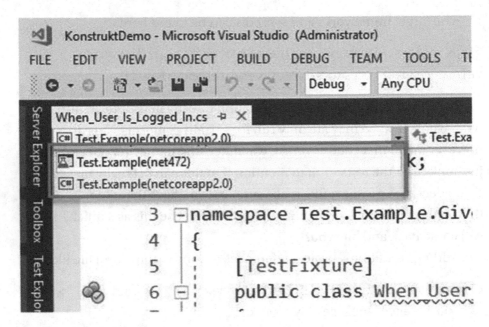

Figure 5-19. *Selecting platform for IntelliSense*

At the time of writing, this is still very buggy and the issue is still open: https://github.com/dotnet/project-system/issues/2733.

In my experience working with conditional compilation can be very messy and frustrating, and I would personally only use this when I had no other choice. And if I had to, I would try to separate the code that differs in different projects, or files, and only use conditional compilation at namespace and reference level.

In an ideal world, your code is scoped to the point where your tests can be migrated a chunk at a time – but we had an intertwined system where even the simplest unit test would need references to all three layers of a service, in addition to the supporting libraries. Therefore, before we migrate the rest of the tests, we would need to sort out the rest of the projects that would be a part of the migration. An alternative, besides conditional compilation (which I've already deemed not a good fit for us), would be to break out tests to separate test projects. As we have some degree of separation, at least per service, we won't have to do that. What we have to do is migrate the rest of the libraries pertaining to the Main service.

Konstrukt.Tenancy

Konstrukt.Tenancy was easy to migrate, only two bigger changes were needed. One of them was replacing the third-party library used for the retry policy for SQL calls with one that supported .NET Standard, Polly. This code was omitted from the source code for brevity as we have already covered how to replace libraries.

The second change was to the classes that used the DbContext type. DbContext creates a dependency on Entity Framework, and besides not wanting to pull in that dependency for just a few methods, we also would have to decide if we want to use Entity Framework Core or Entity Framework .NET. Earlier in the book, I talked about targeting the full framework with ASP.NET Core and how that would allow you to use, for example, Entity Framework .NET. The problem is that according to the ASP.NET Core roadmap, this won't be supported after 3.0. Nonetheless, we don't want EF dependencies in the library that manages the multitenancy logic, and therefore we simply abstract away the context. The ASP.NET Core roadmap can be found here:

```
https://github.com/aspnet/AspNetCore/wiki/roadmap
```

Instead we now inject an IDataStoreContext object that can be used to change the connection string or catalog for the right tenant, while the mapping to a concrete implementation is done in the library that uses it. In Konstrukt. SL.Main we now map IDataStoreContext to a DataStoreContext object.

Migrating to Entity Framework Core

Konstrukt.Entities has to be migrated. Either we migrate to .NET Core, and have all the services use Entity Framework Core, or we can run both side by side – but that can quickly get very messy so we don't want to do that.

Just so you know, you can use Entity Framework Core in .NET libraries, as long as the target framework is newer than 4.61.

We have an additional challenge, besides migrating to EF Core. We are using database first which is not supported, and therefore we need to change this to model first. This means no more EDMX model and scaffolding pain, but some extra pain to get our models set up as they have until this point been scaffolded for us for free.

In the Konstrukt.Entities project, we have our EDMX model and the scaffolded entities (Figure 5-20).

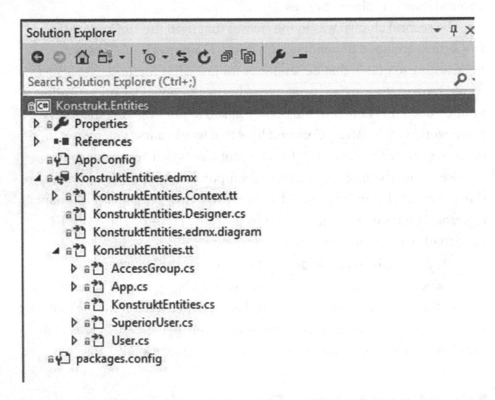

Figure 5-20. *The EDMX model and the scaffolded entities*

EF Core does not support the EDMX model, and there is no plan for supporting this in the future. The model is used to render the designer (Entity Designer) and is used for a database-first approach – an approach that isn't recommended anymore. Instead the model-first approach is recommended, where the model classes you create dictate how the database looks like and behaves. You can however scaffold the entity classes based on an existing database by using the `Scaffold-DbContext` PowerShell cmdlet. This is how we are going to migrate to EF Core from the database-first approach we currently have.

Scaffolding a Database Context

We start off by creating a new .NET Standard project, and we install the EF tools package and our provider:

```
Install-Package Microsoft.EntityFrameworkCore.Tools
Install-Package Microsoft.EntityFrameworkCore.SqlServer
```

Temporarily change the TargetFramework in the csproj to netcoreapp2.0, as the PowerShell cmdlet needs an executable to be able to do the scaffolding.

Set the project as startup project.

Run the following in the Package Manager Console (making sure that you first have navigated to the project).

```
Scaffold-DbContext "Server=AspCoreVM\SQLEXPRESS;;Database=Tena
ntX;Integrated Security=true;" Microsoft.EntityFrameworkCore.
SqlServer -OutputDir Models
```

We should now have the entities scaffolded in the Models folder as shown in Figure 5-21.

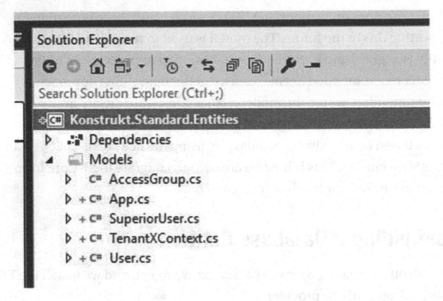

Figure 5-21. Scaffolded entities in the Models folder

Be aware that the connection string is going to be added to the OnConfiguring method – obviously we don't want this. There are a few ways to solve this; you could pull the connection string from a configuration file or use dependency injection. Our solution is a multitenant solution where each tenant has their own database, but for simplicity we are going to pretend like we are only dealing with one database and pull the connection string from a configuration file.

Add the System.Configuration.ConfigurationManager package, a configuration file, and a connection string to the project.

```
protected override void OnConfiguring(DbContextOptionsBuilder
optionsBuilder)
{
    if (!optionsBuilder.IsConfigured)
    {
        var connectionString = ConfigurationManager.Connection
        Strings["KonstruktEntities"].ConnectionString;
```

```
    optionsBuilder.UseSqlServer(connectionString);
    }
}
```

The next step is to update the references in the other projects. Make sure to remove references to Entity Framework .NET and add the right NuGet package in projects where Entity Framework .NET is used. One such example is Konstrukt.DAL.Main as we are referencing the DbContext type in our repository base class. In addition, some other minor fixes are required, such as updating the connection string in the config files from an EF connection string to a plain SQL connection string and changing the way we are retrieving the connection string from the EF context.

From:

```
_context.Database.Connection.ConnectionString
```

To:

```
_context.Database.GetDbConnection().ConnectionString;
```

After verifying that everything builds, the Main service runs, and tests are green, we are ready for the final steps. Migrating the Konstrukt.SL.Main layers, the DAL (data access layer), and the BL (business layer) is done the same way we did with the previous libraries. You might notice that the more libraries you migrate while working your way down the dependency chain, the less work is required. This is the case with the DAL and the BL, and with them migrated it's just as easy to migrate the unit test project as all the references the project has are .NET Standard references.

We are now ready for the final step, and the grand finale – migrating the ASP.NET service Konstrukt.SL.Main to ASP.NET Core.

Migrating from ASP.NET to ASP.NET Core

Create a new ASP.NET Core project targeting .NET Core. As mentioned before, you can target the full .NET Framework, but this will not be supported in the future so we might as well go all the way. We'll break the migration down piece by piece, highlighting common differences.

Service Startup

In ASP.NET Core there is no App_Start folder or Global.asax file as the Startup.cs class manages the startup of the service. All the code pertaining to app service configuration is done in the Startup.cs class, or the Program. cs class (which is executed before the Startup class).

Routing Configuration

In our old project, we mapped the routing in the WebApiConfig class in App_Start by using HttpConfiguration.MapHttpAttributeRoutes. The app. UseMVC() method in the Startup.cs class wires this up for us in ASP.NET Core.

Enabling CORS

Enabling CORS was also done in the WebApiConfig class; this code is moved to the Startup class.

This can be done in two ways. The first way is declaring a CORS policy and then referencing it in a controller by using an attribute:

Startup.cs

```
public void ConfigureServices(IServiceCollection services)
{
    services.AddCors(o => o.AddPolicy("CORSPolicy", builder =>
    {
```

```
        builder.AllowAnyOrigin()
                .AllowAnyMethod()
                .AllowAnyHeader();
    }));
    services.AddMvc().SetCompatibilityVersion(Compatibility
    Version.Version_2_1);
}
```

SomeController.cs

```
[EnableCors("CORSPolicy")]
[HttpGet]
public ActionResult<IEnumerable<string>> Get()
{
    return new string[] { "value1", "value2" };
}
```

Or by applying it globally:

```
public void Configure(IApplicationBuilder app,
IHostingEnvironment env)
{
    app.UseCors("CORSPolicy");

    if (env.IsDevelopment())
    {
        app.UseDeveloperExceptionPage();
    }
    else
    {
        app.UseHsts();
    }

    app.UseHttpsRedirection();
    app.UseMvc();
}
```

Make sure that you add this before app.UseMVC if you add it globally!

Dependency Injection

Dependency injection is at the core of ASP.NET Core (pun intended). While this is a common practice that has been around for a long time, it hasn't been adopted by everybody, although it's accepted as a good practice. I won't go into details as to why, but it helps with maintainability and testability and gives flexibility.

The built-in dependency injection is great, but you can use your own dependency resolver – and we want to keep using Autofac to simplify the migration.

First, we copy over the IOC folder from Konstrukt.SL.Main – which contains the type registration and building of the container. Let's also remember to create the SlimRequest we talked about earlier (when we resolved the missing HttpContext by passing in an abstraction instead), and make sure we wire up all the types we need. That brings up some errors, as we haven't installed Autofac.

Install the Autofac NuGet package as well as the extensions:

```
Install-Package Autofac
Install-Package Autofac.Extensions.DependencyInjection
```

Second, change the ConfigureServices in Startup.cs to return an IServiceProvider, and return from the method an AutofacServiceProvider with a built container passed to its constructor.

We also wire up the context entities:

```
services.AddDbContext<KonstruktEntities>(options =>
options.UseSqlServer(Configuration.GetConnectionString
("Configurations")));
```

This should be the end result:

```
public IServiceProvider ConfigureServices(IServiceCollection
services)
{
    services.AddCors(o => o.AddPolicy("CORSPolicy", builder =>
    {
        builder.AllowAnyOrigin()
            .AllowAnyMethod()
            .AllowAnyHeader();
    }));

 services.AddMvc().SetCompatibilityVersion(CompatibilityVersi
on.Version_2_1);
services.AddDbContext<KonstruktEntities>(options =>
options.UseSqlServer(Configuration.GetConnectionString
("Configurations")));
    var containerBuilder = new ContainerBuilderFactory().
    Create();
    containerBuilder.Populate(services);
    // Register internal types
    containerBuilder.RegisterType<HttpContextAccessor>().
    As<IHttpContextAccessor>();
    return new AutofacServiceProvider(containerBuilder.
    Build());
}
```

Reading Configuration Files

The last bit of code in the WebApiConfig file we need to migrate is the line of code that sets the logging connection string. The connection string is fetched from the Web.config file:

```
LogManager.Configuration.Variables["configurationDb"] =
ConfigurationManager.ConnectionStrings["Configurations"].
ConnectionString;
```

As I mentioned earlier, there is a ConfigurationManager NuGet package that lets you read config files in Core projects, but there is also a new way of working with settings files in ASP.NET Core that is better. Since we used the ConfigurationManager last time, we will look at using a JSON file instead. ASP.NET Core supports different types of configuration providers as seen in Table 5-1.

Table 5-1. *ASP.NET Core Supports Different Types of Configuration Providers*

Provider	Provides Configuration from...
Azure Key Vault Configuration Provider (*Security* Topics)	Azure Key Vault
Command-Line Configuration Provider	Command-line parameters
Custom Configuration Provider	Custom source
Environment Variables Configuration Provider	Environment variables
File Configuration Provider	Files (INI, JSON, XML)
Key-Per-File Configuration Provider	Directory files
Memory Configuration Provider	In-memory collections
User Secrets (Secret Manager) (*Security* Topics)	File in the user profile directory

The providers are configured in the CreateWebHostBuilder method in Program.cs – which is the very first class and method to be executed. The providers are configured in the ConfigureAppConfiguration method:

```
public static IWebHostBuilder CreateWebHostBuilder(string[]
args) =>
    WebHost.CreateDefaultBuilder(args)
        .ConfigureAppConfiguration(config =>
        {
            config.AddJsonFile("appsettings.json", optional:
            false, reloadOnChange: false);
            config.AddXmlFile("Web.config", optional: true,
            reloadOnChange: false);
        })
        .UseStartup<Startup>();
```

The appsettings.json file is read in by default, so if it's the only configuration file you have, you don't need to call the ConfigureAppConfiguration method and pass in the provider for that file.

Since this method is called before ConfigureServices in Startup.cs, you can access the data read with the providers there. This can be done a few ways; one of them is by defining a ConnectionStrings node in the JSON file, with connection string objects.

```
  "AllowedHosts": "*",
  "ConnectionStrings": {
    "Configurations": "db connection"
  },
```

In the Configure method in Startup.cs, you can then access the settings:

```
var dbConnectionString = Configuration.GetConnectionString
("Configurations");
```

You can also use the Options Pattern, and map a settings section to a plain object:

```
"ImportantSettings": {
  "SettingA": "important"
}
```

In Startup.cs:

```
var settings = Configuration.GetSection(nameof(Important
Settings)).Get<ImportantSettings>();
```

You can configure this permanently by registering the mapping in the services collection in the ConfigureServices method in Startup.cs:

```
services.Configure<ImportantSettings>(Configuration.GetSection
(nameof(ImportantSettings)));
```

This means that we can access the settings through dependency injection by passing an IOptions<> object in the constructor of a class that needs them:

```
IOptions<ImportantSettings> settings
```

Sounds familiar? We are actually doing a manual version of this in Konstrukt, with the ISettings (implemented as Settings and using the ConfigurationManager to read the settings).

To summarize this section, the following code

```
LogManager.Configuration.Variables["configurationDb"] =
ConfigurationManager.ConnectionStrings["Configurations"].
ConnectionString;
```

can be replaced by

```
LogManager.Configuration.Variables["configurationDb"] =
Configuration.GetConnectionString("Configurations");
```

Make sure to add the NLog.Web.AspNetCore package to the project as well as NLog.

Let's talk more about logging now that we are done with moving the startup code from the old project to the new one.

Logging

ASP.NET Core has made logging a priority, and I could write a smaller book on that topic. But we'll keep it simple here. Logging is integrated in ASP.NET Core, and it's configured in a similar way to the configuration objects.

There is a variety of providers, and these are configured in the ConfigureLogging method for the WebHostBuilder. By default, these are added:

- Console

- Debug

- EventSource (starting with ASP.NET Core 2.2)

There are many third-party log providers that you can plug in as well. They usually provide an extension method to plug in that provider, and you can do the logging by using dependency injection and the ILoggerFactory.

Previously in this chapter, we used a static instance of our logger in the Logging library to write to the log, but as promised we will now look at using dependency injection instead in our ASP.NET Core app.

We have to do the following things:

1. Add the dependencies.

2. Create a configuration file for NLog.

3. Enable NLog.

Add Dependencies

The two dependencies we need were installed in the previous step:

```
<PackageReference Include="NLog.Web.AspNetCore" Version="4.5.4" />
<PackageReference Include="NLog" Version="4.5.4" />
```

Add NLog Config File

We'll just copy over the NLog config file from the Logging project and make sure that Build Action is set to Content and Copy to Output Directory to Copy always as shown in Figure 5-22.

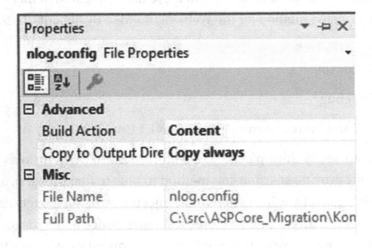

Figure 5-22. *You can set the Copy to Output Directory to Copy always in the Properties window for the file*

Enable NLog

With the configuration file in place, we can enable NLog through the extension method the NLog library provides for the WebHostBuilder in the Program.cs class:

```
public static IWebHostBuilder CreateWebHostBuilder(string[]
args) =>
    WebHost.CreateDefaultBuilder(args)
        .ConfigureAppConfiguration(config =>
        {
            config.AddJsonFile("appsettings.json", optional:
            false, reloadOnChange: false);
            config.AddXmlFile("Web.config", optional: true,
            reloadOnChange: false);
        })
        .UseNLog()
        .UseStartup<Startup>();
```

And we can also go ahead and remove the code that sets the
connection string for NLog from the Startup class, assuming that we now
instead have the connection string in the NLog configuration file:

```
LogManager.Configuration.Variables["configurationDb"] =
Configuration.GetConnectionString("Configurations");
```

By default, the logging level is set in the appsettings.json file, so make
sure the level is the right one. The default logging level when you create a
new project is Warning.

Using the logger is done by passing in ILogger<T> in the constructor
of the class that will make use of the logger. Here is an example using the
ValuesController that is created when you use the default project template
for ASP.NET Core:

```
[Route("api/[controller]")]
[ApiController]
public class ValuesController : ControllerBase
{
    private readonly ILogger<ValuesController> _logger;
```

```
public ValuesController(ILogger<ValuesController> logger)
{
    _logger = logger;
}

[HttpGet]
public ActionResult<IEnumerable<string>> Get()
{
    _logger.LogInformation("GET values called");

    return new string[] { "value1", "value2" };
}
}
```

Authentication

One thing we haven't talked much about in this book is authentication. The authentication service and the code for authenticating users in the services have been omitted from the sample code on purpose as we would rather not expose that. I do want to talk about authentication and authorization, and how it differs when you migrate, as you'll probably need some help one way or another with that.

First of all, it's important to know that authentication is managed in the Startup.cs class, in the Configure services method. This is where you register your identity system configuration by using

```
Services.AddDefaultIdentity
Previous versions of ASP.NET Core used: Services.AddIdentity
```

The difference between the two is that they use different APIs, but they are quite similar, except one difference. AddDefaultIdentity does not add Roles functionality by default. This can be added by calling AddRoles after AddDefaultIdentity.

Example with OpenIdConnect

When you configure services for authentication, you can configure several types, and in our system, we support a variety of ways to authenticate. One of them is OpenIdConnect. Here is an example showing how easy it is to set this up (assuming that you are only using one authority such as Google):

```
public void ConfigureServices(IServiceCollection services)
{
    services.AddAuthentication().AddOpenIdConnect(options =>
    {
        options.ClientId = Configuration["ClientId"];
        options.ClientSecret = Configuration["ClientSecret"];
        options.Authority = Configuration["Authority"];
        options.ResponseType = OpenIdConnectResponseType.Code;
        options.GetClaimsFromUserInfoEndpoint = true;
    });

    services.AddMvc().SetCompatibilityVersion(Compatibility
    Version.Version_2_1);
}
```

appsettings.json:

```
{
  "Logging": {
    "LogLevel": {
      "Default": "Warning"
    }
  },
  "AllowedHosts": "*",
  "ClientId": "",
  "ClientSecret": "",
```

```
   "Authority": ""
}
```

There are many ways to authenticate a user, and covering all the different ways is beyond the scope of this book. But before we move on to the next section, I want to talk about migrating to ASP.NET Core Identity, which unfortunately isn't a straightforward process. We are not using Identity, or Membership, in our system, but I want to highlight some issues that you will come across and how they are best solved. Please refer to the ASP.NET Core documentation for details, as things in this area are going to change in the future.

ASP.NET Core Identity

While there are some similarities between ASP.NET Identity and ASP.NET Core Identity, there are also some significant differences which means that some extra work is required when migrating. You will have to migrate to the new schema, and the recommended way is to migrate the users. For example, there are new columns, and more importantly, the password criteria and hashing have changed.

Here is the same password hashed using ASP.NET Identity:

```
AOstUiMCRZkeV7mQqj4ZygJGtZuKQXxp9Ir+5vQQBikFfGScUcCVYks/
N9E/5zC9Xg==
And hashed in ASP.NET Core Identity
AQAAAAEAACcQAAAAEAYCHwW5NfOnVU84CAhX7xnMEDrXTqq6XO/d7kIv1+HTlcP
felFEgu5mtKEq+LT61A==
```

Microsoft recommends that you leave the password empty after migrating the users to the new schema, and prompt the user to change the password.

Figure 5-23 shows a high-level comparison of the Identity tables created with ASP.NET and ASP.NET Core. There are even differences on column level.

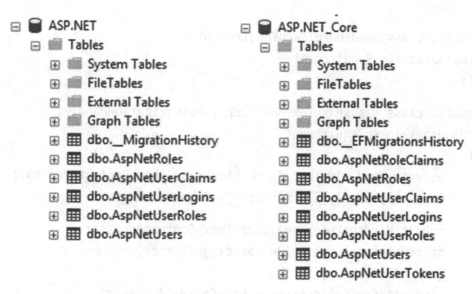

Figure 5-23. *The Identity tables of ASP.NET Core and ASP.NET differ*

Current User

Another change you should be aware of is that there is no ClaimsPrincipal anymore. It represented static state, and that's not something you want. Instead, to access the current user, you can use HttpContext.User (just don't pass around the context! Abstract away the user instead and use dependency injection) or ControllerBase.User in MVC controllers.

Authorization

If you have been using custom authorization attributes in your services, you will need to migrate those as well. In ASP.NET Core the policy pattern, similar to the way you configure CORS policies, is encouraged.

You define a requirement for your policy, implement a handler, register the policy, and then use it.

Here is a simple example from one of our third-party authentication services:

```
public class HandshakeTokenRequirement :
IAuthorizationRequirement
{}

public class HandshakeTokenHandler : AuthorizationHandler
<HandshakeTokenRequirement>
{
    private readonly IHttpContextAccessor _httpContextAccessor;
    private readonly IJwtParser _jwtParser;

    public HandshakeTokenHandler(IHttpContextAccessor
    httpContextAccessor, IJwtParser jwtParser)
    {
        _httpContextAccessor = httpContextAccessor;
        _jwtParser = jwtParser;
    }
    protected override Task HandleRequirementAsync
    (AuthorizationHandlerContext context,
        HandshakeTokenRequirement requirement)
    {
        var httpContext = _httpContextAccessor.HttpContext;

        if (httpContext.Request.Query.
        TryGetValue("handshaketoken", out var handshakeToken)
        && !String.IsNullOrEmpty(handshakeToken))
        {
            if(!_jwtParser.IsValid(handshakeToken))
                context.Fail();
```

```
            // DO stuff, for example - get identity claim

                httpContext.User.AddIdentity(identity);

                context.Succeed(requirement);
            }
        }
        else
        {
            // Log error
            context.Fail();
        }
        return Task.CompletedTask;
    }
}

public class Startup
{
    ...
    public void ConfigureServices(IServiceCollection services)
    {
        ConfigureIoC(services);

        services.AddAuthorization(options =>
        {
            options.AddPolicy(nameof(HandshakeTokenRequirement),
            policy =>
                policy.Requirements.Add(new
                HandshakeTokenRequirement()));
        });
...

[Route("api/[controller]")]
[ApiController]
```

```
public class OauthController : ControllerBase
{
    [HttpGet]
    [Authorize(Policy = nameof(HandshakeTokenRequirement))]
    [Authorize]
    public ActionResult<string> Get(string handshaketoken,
string redirect_uri)
    {
...
```

Migrating Controllers

After setting up our configuration, authentication, and authorization, we only have the controllers left. There is a neat little shim package that we can use to make the migration a little bit easier, the WebApiCompatShim. This shim is only recommended for ASP.NET Core versions up to 3.0. In 3.0 it won't be supported anymore. If you choose to use it nonetheless, install the package:

```
Install-Package Microsoft.AspNetCore.Mvc.WebApiCompatShim
```

Register the shim in Startup.cs:

```
services.AddMvc()
    .SetCompatibilityVersion(CompatibilityVersion.Version_2_1)
    .AddWebApiConventions();
```

Copy over the controllers, update the namespace, and sort out any leftover errors such as fixing references.

RoutePrefix doesn't exist anymore, as the Route attribute acts a route prefix. A Search and Replace as shown in Figure 5-24 takes care of that.

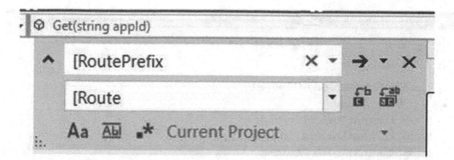

Figure 5-24. *Search and Replace for RoutePrefix*

Import the Route type for all the controllers (Controllers folder) as shown in Figure 5-25.

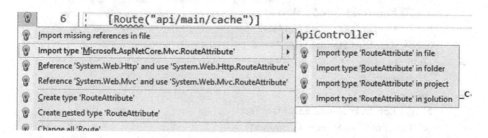

Figure 5-25. *With the help of ReSharper, we can easily fix missing types*

IHttpActionResult is now IActionresult, so another search and replace to fix that.

```
[EnableCors(origins: "*", headers: "*", methods: "*")]
```

The EnableCors attribute is replaced by specifying the CORS policy we registered at startup.

We have now migrated the Main service in full (Figure 5-26)!

119

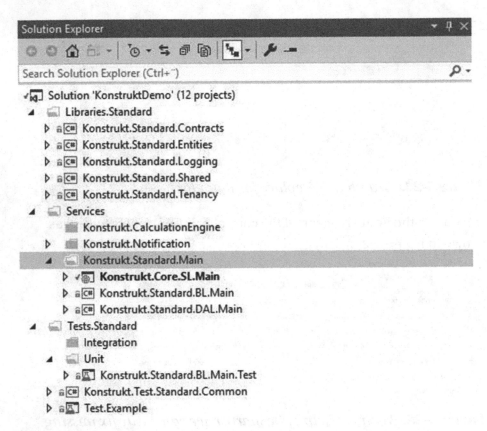

Figure 5-26. *Final result after migrating the Main service*

Static Files

We don't have any static files that we are serving up, but it's not uncommon, and this is how it is done in ASP.NET Core.

Invoke the UseStaticFiles method in Startup.Configuration:

```
public void Configure(IApplicationBuilder app)
{
    app.UseStaticFiles();
}
```

By default, the service will look for static files in the wwwroot folder, but you can change this by configuring where the files reside:

```
public void Configure(IApplicationBuilder app)
{
    app.UseStaticFiles(); // For the wwwroot folder

    app.UseStaticFiles(new StaticFileOptions
    {
        FileProvider = new PhysicalFileProvider(
            Path.Combine(Directory.GetCurrentDirectory(),
"Resources")),
        RequestPath = "/Files"
    });
}
```

There is more to this; you can set cache headers, set MIME types, enable directory browsing, and more. Refer to the documentation for details. But please make sure you don't expose content you don't want to expose, such as your configuration files!

Summary

Whether you're doing a partial or full migration, a good way to start is by migrating the leaves of the dependency graph for a service. The leaves often have less third-party dependencies and therefore theoretically should be easier to migrate. As soon as one library has been migrated, you simply replace the references to the new migrated library and work your way through the dependency graph until everything has been migrated. Since there are no official tools to automagically migrate the code, it has to be done manually. For me, the first few projects took a while to migrate, but honestly, after you have migrated a few projects, you get into the flow and it gets easier. As suggested in this book, make sure that you automate what you can automate by using tools such as ReSharper, built-in Visual Studio tooling, extensions, and simple editor features such as search and replace. Also, one thing that I learned the hard way is to make frequent commits when you do a migration, and to make sure to constantly run the unit tests. There are tools that will run the unit test in the background as soon as anything has changed that affects the tests in question. We decided a while back to not make use of that type of tooling as the performance at the time was horrible, and the tools were unreliable. Visual Studio actually has a feature that will automatically run the unit tests, but we have not used it as we have too many unit tests and therefore cannot use the feature.

Regardless of how you decide on doing the migration, make sure you scope out an area to migrate first, and then do the migration one step at a time. My advice is to be organized and meticulous, and document what you are doing. An excellent way to document is by using frequent source control commits with descriptive messages.

Besides the preceding advice, an equally important thing to consider is the integration and deployment pipeline. Therefore, in the upcoming chapter, we'll take a look at some of the changes we had to make in our pipeline. Most likely your pipeline is going to differ; therefore the purpose of the next chapter is not to give you a blueprint for a pipeline, but rather to prepare you for some of the challenges you might encounter.

CHAPTER 6

Phase 4: Upgrading the Deployment Pipeline

We learned many lessons when we migrated to ASP.NET Core, and one of them was that you might have to make significant changes to your deployment pipeline. If you have a mixed solution, it can get tricky, depending on how the pipeline is set up. In this chapter I want to highlight some changes and challenges that we had.

This chapter is not a guide on how to set up a continuous integration and deployment pipeline. There are many ways to do that and a variety of tools and services to choose between. But one thing I'm sure of is that you will need to change your pipeline when you migrate. And if you have a mixed solution, like we do, you will have additional challenges that you need to solve. In my experience the time and effort that goes into setting up and patching a pipeline is often forgotten when a team is estimating time and effort for migrations. And it can be a lot of work, particularly if you are not prepared. I hope that this chapter will give you some pointers to what sort of challenges you can come across and hopefully some solutions as well.

© Iris Classon 2019

I. Classon, *Migrating ASP.NET Microservices to ASP.NET Core*,
https://doi.org/10.1007/978-1-4842-4327-5_6

Konstrukt Continuous Integration and Deployment Pipeline

When I first set up our pipeline, we were hosting all our services in Azure. We were using something called cloud services for our web services, and virtual machines tied together under a virtual IP. When we moved to a local cloud provider, we changed the setup, but we kept the pipeline – including the tools and steps. The pipeline works like this (Figure 6-1).

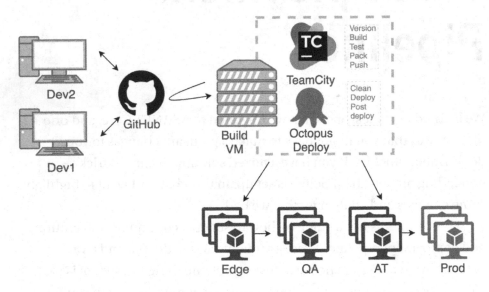

Figure 6-1. *The Konstrukt continuous integration and deployment pipeline works*

The source code is hosted on GitHub (several repositories), and we use Git for our version control. Our development branch is our master branch, and we branch out releases in two-week cycles. For major patches and features, we use temporary branches, but we try to avoid unnecessary branching. Each developer works on their own local copy, committing and pushing changes frequently to the remote repository. Our build machine uses a build service called TeamCity, and the build service listens for changes in the repository. When a commit has been made, it pulls the latest version and goes through a series of build configurations as shown in Figure 6-2, each configuration containing several steps. A build agent is what executes a build configuration, and we have several agents that run in parallel.

Figure 6-2. *Konstrukt build configurations before pushing the packages to the deployment service*

I won't go into the details of the configurations, but this is the process. Our solution is built and run as three separate parts: the client, the web API services, and tools. They all go through the following configurations, and the next configuration is only run if the previous one was successful.

Create Version

We use the build service to set the version number. If the commit was made on a release branch, the version is attached to the end of the version number. This is later parsed and used when we deploy the packages.

Build and Pack

In this step packages are restored, projects are built, and the deployment packages are created (NuGet packages).

Run Unit Tests and Run Integration Tests

The two test types are run as separate configurations as the integration tests rely on a physical database.

Push

Since we deploy all our services at the same time, we need to sync packages, as frontend and backend services are created by different agents. Therefore, in the final step, we make sure that everything was successful and that all the packages created are for the same version. The packages are then pushed to our NuGet server and deployed to either the EDGE server NuGet server or AT (acceptance testing server) – depending on whether this is a release or not.

Deployment Flow

Once the previous steps are finished, Octopus Deploy takes over. Octopus Deploy is our deployment service that manages the deployment to the various environments. Once a package is deployed to the EDGE environment successfully and we can ping all the services, the same packages are then deployed to the QA (quality assurance) environment for manual testing (done by both developers and our testers). Once everything is tested, a release is created by branching out a release branch; the packages are tested in the AT (acceptance testing) environment by testers and early adopters, before being released to production (PROD environment).

The deployment itself of the services is fairly straightforward as seen in Figure 6-3. After some cleanup we deploy the services as IIS web services, with just some minor differences for the ASP.NET Core services.

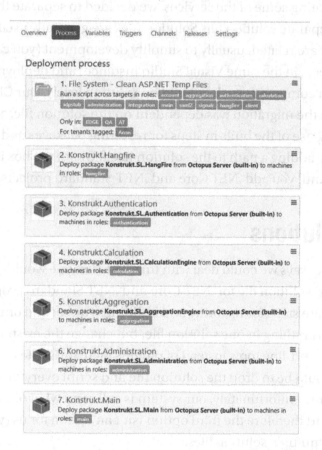

Figure 6-3. Some of the Octopus Deploy deployment steps for Konstrukt

Pipeline Modifications

As I've mentioned before, we've had to make a few changes to our pipeline. The modifications you'll need to make depend on your current setup – and you might end up changing it a few times like we did. When we first started migrating some of the services, we decided to separate the projects by using a separate solution file. Solution files are generally used to group projects that are related, usually to simplify development (you can open related projects in the same Visual Studio instance) and deployment (you can run commands such as build on solution level). Our CI/CD setup before the migration was dependent on the solution file, and we were making use of the built-in steps for restoring packages and building a solution by adding a path to the solution itself. Out of the box it works really well, until you add .NET Core and .NET Standard projects to the mix.

Two Solutions

We had three ways we could deal with this. The first one would be to add a second solution file for .NET Core and .NET Standard projects and create separate steps for restoring and building. The second one would be to have everything in one solution file, but change the existing steps to use command-line tools instead of plugins or TeamCity features. The third way would be to drop the solution file and script everything as in the second option. Unfortunately, our system is still somewhat of a distributed monolith, and therefore the third option isn't an option for us (yet). We decided on multiple solution files.

CLI First

.NET Core has a command-line-first approach, with excellent CLI tooling. TeamCity recommends that you use their .NET Core plugin for restoring packages and building and creating deployment packages. At the time the plugin had several issues; one of them was that it didn't support wildcard selection of multiple projects for restoring packages and building the assemblies. Adding a separate step for each build would be a pain to maintain, and it didn't work with mixed projects in a solution if you targeted the solution file. With separate solution files, we could run the restore or build command targeting Konstrukt.Core.sln. Moving forward we started consolidating the steps and moved away from built-in features and favored scripting the steps instead (by using native CLI tools instead of plugins).

Creating NuGet Packages

Our deployment packages are NuGet packages that are created as a part of the build process by using a NuGet package from Octopus Deploy that creates the packages upon build by using NuGet.exe behind the scenes. We've had this setup since the beginning, but unfortunately this tool does not support .NET Core projects. As we had two separate solutions, we decided to keep the build step for Konstrukt.sln (.NET) with the "Run OctoPack" option enabled. For Konstrukt.Core.sln we used a PowerShell script to create the packages by using octo.exe. You can create packages automagically upon build, by simply adding GeneratePackageOnBuild set to true in the project file. We needed additional tweaks and opted out of that option and instead wrote our own script.

Running Tests

We ran into problems with our tests as well. All our tests (for the back end) use NUnit, and we had been using the NUnit Console Runner – which unfortunately does not currently support .NET Core. At the time of writing, they are considering a separate runner, but it is still in the planning stages. Therefore, we used the "dotnet test" command instead, which in earlier versions of .NET Core SDK had a bug when you targeted the solution file and would yield errors instead of skipping projects that were not test projects. This has fortunately been fixed now.

The takeaway is that you will most likely need to maintain separate steps, and the easiest way to consolidate similar steps is by scripting the steps instead of relying on plugins and built-in features. I'm sure this depends on the build service that you are using, but generally I've found that GUI-driven tools and services are slower to adopt changes and can be very limiting.

Deploying

Deploying required the least amount of work for us. We decided on not creating self-contained packages as we don't need to run multiple versions side by side, and we would rather keep the deployment packages small. We are also using IIS for our services and will continue to do so until we deploy to a different operating system. The changes we had to make were to make sure we had the IIS module installed (.NET Core Hosting Bundle) and set the .NET CLR version to No Managed Code. We created two separate templates in Octopus Deploy, one for our "old" services and one for ASP.NET Core services. If you deploy self-contained packages and use the in-process hosting model, you will need to disable the app pool for 32-bit (x86) processes. Don't forget to make sure that the identity used for the process has the required permissions. We have a separate account for all our deployment services and have set up our deployment steps in Octopus Deploy to use that identity.

Summary

One of the lessons we learned the hard way is that you can spend significant amount of time adjusting the pipeline for a mixed deployment or a new deployment pipeline. The amount of time required depends on several factors, such as the flexibility of the tools and services you use, the size of the solution, and rigidness of the setup, among other things. Keep this in mind as you prepare a migration, and adjust the pipeline as soon as you have something that builds so you can run your build process early on to avoid the common "it builds on my machine" problem, not to mention the disappointing surprise that you might have to spend a fair bit of time fixing a broken pipe.

CHAPTER 7

Maintenance and Resources

When we migrated, we did so enthusiastically and naively. Future technical debt in our ASP.NET Core services wasn't on our mind (they were brand new after all!), and we certainly didn't spend a lot of energy thinking and planning maintenance. Then a new version on ASP.NET Core came out, and suddenly we had a lot of work to do if we wanted to stay up to date. We lagged behind two versions when we did the second migration, and there were several breaking changes that had been announced well in advance – that we could have been prepared for.

A poorly planned and unmanaged migration can cause problems with technical debt in the future. This goes for all code we write, not only when we migrate to something new and juicy. However, in my experience, the excitement and challenge of migrating to something new make it easy to forget to plan ahead. In the next few pages, I'd like to give some advice, and some resources, that can reduce future technical debt, and hopefully make this journey a smoother ride.

© Iris Classon 2019
I. Classon, *Migrating ASP.NET Microservices to ASP.NET Core*,
https://doi.org/10.1007/978-1-4842-4327-5_7

Framework Changes

I mentioned in one of the first chapters that one of the possible downsides of open source frameworks is that they frequently change – and breaking changes aren't unheard of. You probably use some team collaboration software to communicate with the team, and be that Slack or Teams (or other), I recommend that you set up alerts and notifications for the Core repositories.

Slack has a plugin that lets you easily subscribe to a repository, but there is always the option of using web hooks (custom callbacks to a URL based on a trigger). This is supported by most collaboration tools, including Microsoft Teams: `https://docs.microsoft.com/en-us/microsoftteams/platform/concepts/connectors/connectors-using`

Read more about Slack integration here: `https://github.com/integrations/slack`

The web hooks support a variety of triggers: `https://developer.github.com/webhooks/`

You can also subscribe by email, and you can also only subscribe to new releases as shown in Figure 7-1. If you use an unfiltered subscribe expect a lot of noise – and consider applying a filter.

Figure 7-1. *GitHub lets you subscribe to a repository for all notifications or releases only*

You might also want to take a look at the support policy for the different versions of the framework if you're using an older version. You can find the support policy here: `https://dotnet.microsoft.com/platform/support/policy`

Announcements and Roadmaps

In the previous section, I mentioned subscribing to repositories, and the ASP.NET team has made it even easier for us to stay up to date by creating an announcement repository (Figure 7-2). If you subscribe to it, you will be notified on all issues and surrounding discussions. The issues have tags for

"Announcement", "Breaching change", and the version numbers for easy searching.

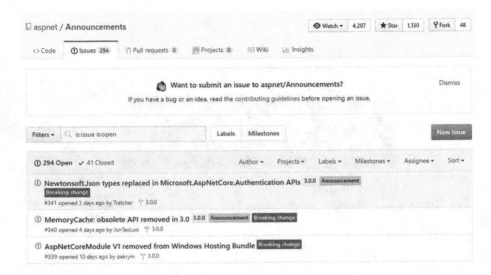

Figure 7-2. *The Announcements repository is where you can find announcements and breaking changes*

In the ASP.NET Core repository, you can find the roadmap in the Wiki (Figure 7-3). Although slim, it should be fairly up to date. Besides a high-level overview, it also contains links for more information.

Figure 7-3. *The ASP.NET Core roadmap can be found on GitHub*

Entity Framework Core roadmap is located in the documentation – and not under the Wiki for the repo. The Wiki does however have the link to the roadmap and other useful links. The roadmap can be found here: `https://docs.microsoft.com/en-us/ef/core/what-is-new/roadmap`

Documentation

Before I move on to the next piece of advice, I'd like to add a side note on documentation. Although the Microsoft documentation is sourced from different places, not just GitHub, you'll find a lot of the relevant documentation on GitHub. You could in theory subscribe to the repository and be notified of changes – but bear in mind that not everything is going to be relevant and it might instead create a lot of noise. You can find the documentation repository here: `https://github.com/aspnet/Docs`

Align Architecture with New Conventions

Throughout the book we've talked about conventions. Moving forward I would recommend that you and your team try as much as possible to align your architecture with the new conventions that you decide to take on board. There are different ways to do this, but usually some sort of analyzer/linting tool can be helpful. There are numerous Roslyn Code Analyzers that integrate directly with the compiler, for example, the Microsoft.ASPNETCore.MVC.APi.Analyzers (included in ASP.NET Core 2.2) that yields warnings when an API doesn't follow a recommended set of rules. It was introduced with ASP.NET Core 2.2, but works with 2.1 as well. I won't go into details, but have a read here if you want to learn more: `https://docs.microsoft.com/en-us/aspnet/core/web-api/advanced/analyzers`

.NET Standard

As the system grows and you add new projects for services, tools, and libraries, target .NET Standard as much as possible to ensure future compatibility. Unless you need something really obscure, there really isn't any reason as to why you wouldn't want to make a new library a .NET Standard library. By making it a .NET Standard library, you keep your options open.

Test, Test, and Then Test Some More

With test-friendly conventions such as dependency injection and modular architecture, ASP.NET Core is unit and integration test-friendly. In the 2.1 release, Microsoft also released a testing package, Microsoft.AspNetCore.Mvc.Testing. It lets you host the full web stack in memory while providing a test client. This includes a database. You don't have to worry about network or database setups (which have been a pain for us to be honest!), and you can test the full application stack. Besides the testing package, you can also find that ASP.NET Core has introduced several objects that simplify unit testing, not just integration testing. For example, tests involving a HttpContext is easily mocked with the DefaultHttpContext object.

Community Resources and Tools

.NET Core is command-line oriented which has made it easier for the community to create tooling that fits with the .NET Core SDK. Here are some of my favorite tools, and packages, that can make our life easier. Some of them have been mentioned earlier in the book.

Dotnet Templates

You can find useful (and timesaving) dotnet templates at `https://dotnetnew.azurewebsites.net/`. I've used the NUnit test templates (before creating my own) and various ASP.NET Core SPA templates. Creating your own templates for .NET Core is not hard and can be very useful particularly in a team where not everybody is comfortable starting from scratch. This documentation guides you through the few steps needed to create a custom template: `https://docs.microsoft.com/en-us/dotnet/core/tutorials/create-custom-template`

Portability Analyzer

The Portability Analyzer analyzes a project's portability to .NET Core and Standard. You can find the tool and more information here: `https://docs.microsoft.com/en-us/dotnet/standard/analyzers/portability-analyzer`

Windows Compatibility Pack

If you need a shim for .NET Framework–only APIs so you can port code to a .NET Standard library and still be able to compile, you can use the NuGet package Windows Compatibility Pack: `www.nuget.org/packages/Microsoft.Windows.Compatibility`

.NET Core Test Explorer for Visual Studio Code

If you would like a Test Explorer similar to the one in Visual Studio, but for Visual Studio Code, you can use the .NET Core Test Explorer: `https://marketplace.visualstudio.com/items?itemName=formulahendry.dotnet-test-explorer`

C# for Visual Studio Code

For C# editing support, lightweight development, and debugging tools for .NET Core, you can use the popular C# extension: `https://marketplace.visualstudio.com/items?itemName=ms-vscode.csharp`

Crowdsourced Tools and Frameworks

Thang Chung maintains a popular crowdsourced list of awesome tools and frameworks for .NET Core: `https://github.com/thangchung/awesome-dotnet-core`

Crowdsourced .NET Core Global Tools

Nate McMaster has a repository that contains a list of .NET Core Global Tools, such as tools for creating dacpac files, managing certificates, cleaning a solution, command-line HTTP servers, and more: `https://github.com/natemcmaster/dotnet-tools`

If you are interested in building your own .NET Core Global Tool, have a read here: https://docs.microsoft.com/en-us/dotnet/core/tools/global-tools

Stay Up to Date

At this point you might have noticed that a lot of the advice here is to combat the downsides listed early in the book. One of them was that it can get overwhelming for developers to stay up date. Here are some additional resources for staying up to date.

Microsoft Blogs

Web development: https://blogs.msdn.microsoft.com/webdev/

Dotnet: https://blogs.msdn.microsoft.com/dotnet/

Developer tools: https://blogs.msdn.microsoft.com/developer-tools/

Not official Microsoft blogs, but relevant nonetheless:

Hanselman (mixed Microsoft content): www.hanselman.com/blog/

Dotnet Foundation: www.dotnetfoundation.org/blog

Podcast

OnDotnet: https://channel9.msdn.com/Shows/On-NET

The .NET Core Podcast (not Microsoft): https://dotnetcore.show/

Live StandUps

.NET Community StandUps: www.twitch.tv/events/RNn48aCNTZ6wOSQET48uOg

ASP.NET Community StandUp: https://live.asp.net/

Twitter

ASP.NET: `https://twitter.com/aspnet`

.NET: `https://twitter.com/DotNet`

.NET Foundation: `https://twitter.com/dotnetfdn`

The accounts can also be found on Facebook.

Forums

Dotnet Foundation: `https://forums.dotnetfoundation.org/`

ASP.NET Forum: `https://forums.asp.net/`

Gitter ASP.NET: `https://gitter.im/aspnet/Home`

Gitter Dotnet community: `https://gitter.im/dotnet/community`

Note   Gitter is a messaging and collaboration forum centered around GitHub projects.

Videos (General)

MS Build and Ignite videos are great resources. You can find them on Channel 9 under events: `https://channel9.msdn.com/Events/Build`

Video Training

If you want or need to do some technical training, you can find many official resources. Although there are many technical training providers, I would still recommend taking a look at what Microsoft has to offer first, as they are often a step ahead with new content. Besides the documentation, which contains tutorials for most frameworks and tools, there is Microsoft

Learn – which among other things incorporates what used to be called Microsoft Virtual Academy. You'll find plenty of hands-on tutorials there and other resources.

Summary

Maintenance and technical debt are not easy topics. Being a startup, we struggle balancing new features for investors and clients with managing our growing system in such a way that we don't accumulate technical debt faster than we can manage it. Besides the advice I've given in this chapter, we've also done a few other things that aren't platform or framework specific. We are an agile team and work in sprints, and we alternate our sprints with sprints that are feature heavy and hot fixes and sprints where the focus is on technical depth, refactoring, and bugs. Our product is in perpetual beta, which essentially means that the production version is always in an open beta and the clients participate in testing and giving feedback. Our developers are involved with support, first-, second-, and third-line support. We have biweekly architectural discussions and do full-day retrospectives after each sprint. Although we aren't doing a lot of pair programming, we do have a rotating schedule for doing code reviews (so we alternate who is reviewing who), and we get everybody involved in the issues for the sprint. The daily standups help us stay connected, even when some of us work from home or work a different schedule. However, these things alone are not enough.

The work you put in before accumulating the debt matters a lot. Therefore, when you're doing a migration, use the opportunity to embrace a more flexible and maintainable architecture as the one ASP.NET Core promotes, stay up to date and engaged, test thoroughly, and use the available tools and resources.

I've done my very best to share with you the lessons I learned from migrating. When we started migrating, there was very little information about the topic, and even as I'm wrapping up this book years later, I cannot find any real-world migration examples documented. I understand that your situation is going to differ, and that everything I recommend might not work for you, but I sincerely hope that this book has made it easier for you and answered the majority of your questions. If you have questions left unanswered, do reach out to me, and I'll make sure to find some answers for you. I would also like to remind you that the Microsoft teams behind ASP.NET Core and .NET Core are not unreachable, and in my experience, they have been very helpful and accommodating when I've had questions.

ASP.NET Core and .NET are here to stay so make sure that you stay engaged with the community and the team. For many of us, programming is more than just a job – it's a passion that spans beyond our workday as evidenced by the busy repositories on GitHub. Community user groups, such as those found on MeetUp, `www.meetup.com/`, can be a great place to meet like-minded people or to learn new things.

Index

A, B

Acceptance testing (AT), 11, 20, 126

Administration service, 6

AggregationEngine, 6

Analysis, projects preparation

    cost of migration, 53, 54

    details tab, 49, 50

    ICanHasDot.Net, 51, 52

    Konstrukt.BL.Main, 50, 51

    portability summary

        Autofac, 47

        dynamitey library, 47

        EF, 47, 48

        Log4Net, 48

        Microsoft.

          ApplicationInsights, 49

    retargeting, 31–34

    SL.Main dependency

        diagram, 30

    unused references,

        removing, 39–45

    unused types and members,

        removing, 35–39

Application Performance

    Management (APM) tool, 49

Architecture alignment, 138

Architecture, Konstrukt

    administration, 6

    AggregationEngine, 6

    authentication, 6

    CalculationEngine, 7

    decoupling and failure

        resistance, 5

    microservices, 4

    NoSQL databases, 4

    NotificationService, 7

Architecture plan

    conventions, 60, 61

    migrate

        ASP.NET Core, 56

        ASP.NET services, 56

        logical parts to new

          services, 58, 59

        .NET Standard, 56

        OpenIdConnect

          authentication, 57

        SAML authentication, 57

        whole services, 58

    resources, 55, 56

ASP.NET Core *vs.* ASP.NET tag, 21

ASP.NET Identity, 114

Authentication service, 6, 112

Autofac, 47, 104

T, U, V

W, X, Y, Z

Printed in the United States
By Bookmasters